RICHARD NIXON

RICHARD NIXON

RISE AND FALL OF A PRESIDENT

REBECCA LARSEN

Franklin Watts
New York/London/Toronto/Sydney
1991

Library of Congress Cataloging-in-Publication Data

Larsen, Rebecca.
  Richard Nixon : rise and fall of a president / by Rebecca Larsen.
    p.   cm.
  Includes bibliographical references and index.
  Summary: Traces the life and political career of the thirty-
seventh president, from his student days, through the Watergate
scandal which cost him the presidency, to his retirement and new
career as a writer.
  ISBN 0-531-10997-6
  1. Nixon, Richard M. (Richard Milhous), 1913–   —Juvenile
literature.   2. Presidents—United States—Biography—Juvenile
literature.   3. United States—Politics and government—1945—
Juvenile literature.   [1. Nixon, Richard M. (Richard Milhous),
1913–   .   2. Presidents.]   I. Title.
E856.L37   1991
973.924′092—dc20
[B]
[92]   90-23828   CIP   AC

CONTENTS

CHAPTER ONE

A SERIOUS STUDENT

T H E small frame cottage on a knoll overlooking a lemon grove in Yorba Linda, California, was warm and cozy on the night of January 9, 1913. Francis A. Nixon, best known to family and friends as Frank, had two wood stoves burning so that the warmth would fill the master bedroom where his wife, Hannah, was giving birth to her second child. A doctor and nurse got there in time for the arrival of the 11-pound (5-kg) roly-poly boy with thick dark hair.

His mother named the baby Richard, after Richard the Lionhearted, and gave him her family's name, Milhous, as his middle name. From the start, Richard was known for his loud scream, and his grandmother Milhous was sure it meant he would be a preacher or a teacher.

The Nixons already had another son, Harold, four, and by the time Richard was two, he had another brother, Donald.

The Nixon family's lemon farm was set in Orange County, about 30 miles (48 km) from Los Angeles, an area where farmers grew avocados and citrus, barley and alfalfa. In spring the scent of citrus blossoms filled the air, and wildflowers—California poppies, mustard, lupin, and violets—carpeted the hillsides. But it was also a wild, rough land of cactus, rattlesnakes, and tumbleweeds. Sometimes, howling hot winds turned the air to dust, and winters could be chilly and damp.

Few families lived in the area when the Nixons moved in.

Still Richard Nixon found much to excite him in Yorba Linda as a child—"glimpses of the Pacific Ocean to the west, the San Bernardino Mountains to the north, a 'haunted house' in the nearby foothills to be viewed with awe."[1]

Most exotic of all was a railroad line about a mile (1.6 km) away where steam engines puffed by. At night in bed, he awoke to hear train whistles and thought about faraway cities and countries. "All through grade school my ambition was to become a railroad engineer," he said.[2]

Yorba Linda was mostly Quaker and so was Richard's mother, Hannah, who was known for her quiet, hardworking personality and deep religious faith. She had been part of an Irish Quaker family, the Milhouses, who moved from Indiana to Whittier, California, in 1897.

She attended Whittier College for two years, and then became a schoolteacher. A slender, almost gloomy-looking young woman, she had a prominent, jutting nose that her son Richard inherited. In spite of her solemn appearance, when Frank Nixon met her at a church social gathering, he was impressed. "I immediately stopped going with the five other girls I was dating," he said, "and saw Hannah every night."[3]

Hannah's parents and eight brothers and sisters advised her not to marry Frank Nixon, who was ambitious and intelligent but had little schooling and a lowly job as a ranchhand. Not only that, his strong and loud personality upset the calm, deep-thinking Quakers. "He was very unlike my birthright relatives, who were quiet, subdued, inclined to see both sides of every question," said Richard Nixon's cousin, the writer Jessamyn West. "Frank saw one side: his; and he was not bashful about letting you know what was wrong with your side."[4]

But Hannah and Frank kept courting, and after a few months they married, on June 25, 1908. Eventually, they saved enough money to buy their small lemon ranch in Yorba Linda. But the land had poor soil. When his crop of lemons fell short, Frank had to work part-time as a local handyman, doing carpentry and electrical work.

Despite Frank's rough manners, the Nixons fitted in easily to the mostly Quaker community. Frank, formerly a Methodist, converted to the Quaker church and became a Sunday-school teacher and hard worker in the church.

The Nixon family's life focused tightly on their church. There were daily prayers and Bible readings and sometimes as many as four services to attend on Sunday.

It was unusual for the soft-spoken Hannah Nixon to spank her children. She was more likely to sit them down for a serious talk. But Frank could be loud and very physical, as one incident from Richard Nixon's childhood proved.

A dangerous irrigation canal ran very close to the Nixon cottage, and the Nixon children were forbidden to play near it or swim in its 2 or 3 feet (0.6–0.9 m) of water. Once, Frank caught Richard and Harold paddling in the channel and pulled them out and then threw them back in again, shouting, "Do you like water? Have some more of it!"[5]

His father's quick temper made a strong impression on Richard, and he quickly learned not to upset him. "He was a strict and stern disciplinarian, and I tried to follow my mother's example of not crossing him when he was in a bad mood," Nixon has said.[6]

When Richard was five, Hannah had another baby, Arthur, whose life had a deep influence on Richard as the years passed.

At age six, already reading, Richard set off for first grade in a starched white shirt, big black bow tie and knee pants. Like most of the students, in warm weather he went barefoot. His mother told his teachers to call him by his full first name, Richard (by the time he got to high school, he was using the nickname Dick).

To his first teacher, Mary George Skidmore, he almost seemed born with knowledge inside his head. "He had only to be exposed or shown, and he never forgot," she said.[7]

Because of his photographic memory and his quiet study habits, he skipped second grade. He was known as a bookworm, although he joined in baseball and football games. He also loved newspapers, and magazines like the *National Geographic* and *Saturday Evening Post.*

Once while staying at a relative's house, he lay on the floor and read newspaper stories about the Teapot Dome oil scandal, government corruption that took place under President Warren Harding. He told an aunt, "When I grow up, I'm going to be an honest lawyer so things like that can't happen."[8]

Because he showed some early musical talent, eleven-year-old Richard went to live with his aunt Jane Beeson in Lindsay, California, where he had daily piano lessons and also studied violin with a nearby teacher. But a musical career was not to be. Later, as president, he took this same aunt to hear pianist Andre Watts play. His aunt told him: "If thee had practiced more on the piano, thee could be down there now on the stage instead of up here."[9]

After school, Richard and his brothers hoed weeds and dug irrigation ditches in the lemon grove, but in spite of the labor of the whole family, Frank Nixon could never make the farm produce. So in 1922, the Nixons moved to Whittier, where Frank opened a service station and a general store and market.

The whole family worked in the store, and sometimes they didn't even have time to eat together. The burden seemed especially heavy on Hannah Nixon, who saved over-ripe fruit from the store and woke each morning at three or four to bake fruit pies that sold for 35¢ each. She had to handle most of the customers as well, because Frank seemed to irritate them. The boys and their mother tried to keep him away from the counters, where he yelled when he got angry or argued politics. He voted mainly Republican but had strong ideas about the rights of the working man.

Like his father, Richard enjoyed political discussions and soon became a champion debater in school. In his first debate, in seventh grade, he won by arguing the yes side of the proposition "It is more economical to rent a house than to own one."

In 1925, tragedy struck the Nixon household when Arthur, the youngest, fell ill. Gradually, he weakened until, in August that year, he died of what the doctor said was encephalitis or tubercular meningitis.

The family was hard hit. Frank Nixon believed that the death might be some judgment by God because he had been keeping his business open on Sundays. From then on, he kept it closed.

Dick fell into a deep silence. "For weeks after Arthur's funeral there was not a day that I did not think about him and cry," he later said.[10]

Not long after Arthur's death, Dick spotted a woman shoplifting in the family store. His mother soon saw her slip food items under her coat three days in a row. What should she do next, she wondered, because the customer came from a well-known family and her sons went to school with Dick. Frank wanted her arrested, but Dick said, "Let's drop the whole thing. You know what it will do to those boys to learn that their mother is a thief. Work it out some other way."

When Hannah confronted the woman the next day, she confessed and asked to be allowed to pay a little each month until her debt was repaid. "My husband thought the woman would never pay us back," Hannah said. "But Richard was sure I had done the right thing. It took months and months, but eventually she paid us every cent. Richard *was* right."[11]

What made Arthur's death especially painful for the Nixons was that Dick's older brother, Harold, had also developed tuberculosis. While Dick was the serious, hardworking son, Harold was the handsome, popular one who made friends easily and loved daring adventures like flying airplanes and racing his Model T Ford. Although their personalities differed, the two brothers were very close.

Frank scraped together the money to send Harold to a costly private sanatorium, which was then considered the best treatment for the lung disease. Harold improved but then got worse, and by then the family's money was running out. Still hoping for a cure, Hannah took Harold to live in the dry mountain climate of Prescott, Arizona, 800 miles (1,300 km) from Whittier. She rented a small cabin and took in three other TB patients. For almost three years, she served as their nurse, cleaning their bedpans, giving them bed baths and alcohol rubs.

A SERIOUS STUDENT

Meanwhile, Frank, Don, and Dick lived alone except for weekend and summertime visits to Harold and Hannah. By then, Dick was in high school, first at Fullerton High and then at Whittier High beginning in his junior year.

In high school he threw himself into his studies and also into football, basketball, and track. He was not good at sports, but he loved them. "He was persistent and he tried with every ounce of strength he had, but he just didn't seem to have the feel for it," said James Grieves, a high school classmate.[12] Finally, Dick made the second-string team in football. He also participated on the debate team and in speech contests.

Dick's school activities were only part of a grueling daily grind. He still had to carry his weight in the family store, and as soon as he could drive, he woke each morning at four to buy produce at the farmer's market in Los Angeles and then returned home to set up the vegetables for the day.

"Studious," "serious," "persistent" were all words that Dick's classmates used to describe him. But his hard work and ambition left him little time for making close friends, or even for just having a good time or showing signs of teenage rebellion. It was a side of his personality for which he would be criticized all his life. When he became an adult, some people would see his ambition and persistence as somehow cold and inhuman.

His first-grade teacher thought his Quaker upbringing played a part in it. "Quakers are quite strict, and he was strictly brought up to mind and to do this and to do that. He understood what he was at school for. He was there to learn and not to play around," said Mary George Skidmore.[13]

Fellow high school student James Grieves found him a little bit reserved but still interested in making friends. "But I think he was probably more serious and more dedicated than most of us were at that time," he said.[14]

Even so, Dick did have a high school sweetheart, Ola Florence Welch. In his senior year, the two of them appeared in a play sponsored by the Whittier Latin teachers. It was based on the *Aeneid,* the poem by the ancient Roman poet

Virgil. Dick played the Roman hero Aeneas, and Ola played Queen Dido, Aeneas's lover. For Dick, the performance was torture. He had to force size 9 boots on his 11-D feet and then, when he embraced Dido in her death scene, his classmates hooted and hollered. "Virgil obviously had not written the *Aeneid* for a high school assembly in Whittier, California," he later noted.[15]

Dick and Ola dated throughout high school and college, but they were a stormy pair. "He'd be harsh and I'd cry and then we'd make up," she said.[16]

As a junior, Dick also made his first try at politics. He ran for president of the student body and lost to a more popular student, a football and basketball star. After the election, Dick was appointed manager of the student body by the faculty and took charge of selling football tickets and ads in the school yearbook.

At the end of his senior year, Dick received the Harvard Club of California's award for outstanding all-around student. The award brought him a scholarship, and there was also the possibility that he could have gotten a scholarship to Yale. But it was the depths of the Depression, and the Nixon family was still bearing the heavy load of Harold's illness. Hannah Nixon also had given birth to another son, Edward, shortly before Dick's graduation.

So instead, Dick had to live at home and attend Whittier College, where his grandfather had set up a tuition scholarship for all his grandchildren. Whittier was a good Quaker school, but it lacked the glamor of Ivy League schools like Harvard and Yale.

Later in life, Dick claimed that he was not disappointed at losing his chance to study on the East Coast, even though he had spent so much time as a child daydreaming about visits to far-off places. He wrote in his memoirs, "The idea of college was so exciting that nothing could have dimmed it for me."[17]

CHAPTER TWO

A DRIVE TO WIN

T H E seventeen-year-old Nixon who entered college in the fall of 1930 was a slender youth of about 150 pounds (68 kg) still viewed by his friends as a very serious person. But his smile was engaging and friendly when he chose to use it. His curly dark hair was swept back from his forehead the way he would wear it the rest of his life. Although his nose had the ski-jump shape that one day inspired many cartoons and jokes, he of course had not yet developed the heavy jowls of middle age.

In some ways going to Whittier College must have been an easy change for Nixon. The school had only 400 students and many had gone to Whittier High. Yet there was more competition in the classroom than he had experienced before, even though he earned A's and B's. "For the first time I met students who were able to get good grades without working very hard for them, but I needed the steady discipline of nightly study to keep up with all the courses and reading," he later wrote.[1]

The tree-shaded campus on a hillside had been founded by Quakers but was nonsectarian by the time Nixon got there, even though chapel was required three times a week and there was no smoking or dancing on campus. John Greenleaf Whittier, after whom the school and the town were named, was a nineteenth-century Quaker poet who fought against slavery and for the vote for women. He was also one of the founders of the Republican Party. The school's teams were called the Poetlings in honor of Whittier's verse.

Although many professors were Quakers, they encouraged the students to challenge some of the principles with which they had been raised and to investigate new ideas.

Nixon especially admired Dr. Paul Smith, his history teacher, who later became president of the college, a man who introduced the students to new ways of thinking about history and the Constitution. He pointed out to them some of the faults and flaws of the nation's Revolutionary heroes.

Smith thought highly of Nixon and found that Nixon was good at analyzing topics but not too good at philosophizing about them. Sometimes his essay exams seemed almost too brief to Smith. "I would read the paper and feel that it wasn't sufficient for the top grading. But, in looking back to what was left out, nothing was left out so far as the examination question itself was asking for something," Smith said.[2]

In another course, The Philosophy of Christian Reconstruction, some of Nixon's ideas about God were shaken. His parents had raised him to believe completely in the Bible. But in this class, he wrote an essay "What Can I Believe?" in which he said Jesus was the Son of God, but not necessarily in the physical sense of the term. It didn't matter whether the resurrection was true or not, he said. "The important fact is that Jesus lived and taught a life so perfect that he continued to live and grow after his death—in the hearts of men."[3]

No Greek fraternities or sororities were allowed at Whittier but there was a men's club, the Franklins, largely made up of wealthy students who had high social status on campus. Nixon and one of his friends were upset at the snobbish Franklins and decided to start their own club.

A professor agreed to sponsor the new group, which was called the Orthogonians, a word which means right-angled or upright. Members were mostly athletes and those working their way through college, and the group had a rowdy, masculine flavor. "The Franklins posed for their yearbook pictures wearing tuxedos; we posed for our pictures wearing open-necked shirts," Nixon said.[4]

Members said they were dedicated to the four B's: Beans, Brawn, Brains, and Bowels. Their symbol was a boar's head, which led some students to call them "the big pigs."[5]

Nixon wrote the group's constitution, initiation rites, and song, and even though he was a freshman he was elected its first president. He also recruited as a member a star athlete who was black, William Brock, and ever after, Brock was Nixon's friend. "I get really mad when I hear Democrats or anybody accuse him of bigotry. . . . Dick was my buddy in college many years before he or anybody else figured him to become a politician," Brock said.[6]

In his freshman year, Nixon was also elected president of his class and president of the History Club. He entered debate and speech contests, sang in the glee club, and performed in school plays. "He was a lad who also spread himself out tremendously," said Paul Smith. "He was into everything."[7]

Some have wondered whether Nixon threw himself into the college merry-go-round as a way of forgetting a serious family crisis—at home, Harold was sinking steadily toward death.

One day in March 1933, near the end of Nixon's junior year, Harold asked his brother to drive him downtown so that he could buy a new electric mixer for his mother's birthday. Harold was weak and tired during the visit to the hardware store. When the two brothers got home, they hid the mixer on a high closet shelf.

The next morning, Nixon went off to college and was studying in the library when he got an urgent message from home. When he arrived, an undertaker was taking Harold's body away. "That night I got the cake mixer out and gave it to my mother and told her that it was Harold's gift to her," Nixon later wrote.[8]

Although Nixon had never been outstanding at high school sports, he still tried out for football at Whittier. He was destined to be a bench warmer. "The only times I got to play were in the last few minutes of a game that was already safely won or hopelessly lost."[9]

But he still loved the team and was always ready to play in scrimmage games or to help others who needed to work out. When someone on the team was injured, said Charles Kendle, a former teammate, "The first guy that talked to this person would be Dick. Dick would be over giving him a pep talk."[10]

Although he didn't start, Dick became withdrawn and nervous before games, so much so that he couldn't sleep or eat very well. Throughout his life, this was his pattern in times of crisis.

Nixon admired the dynamic, demanding coach of the Poetlings, Wallace "Chief" Newman, who was part American Indian. "He believed in always playing cleanly, but he also believed that there is a great difference between winning and losing. He used to say 'Show me a good loser, and I'll show you a loser,' " Nixon said.[11]

The same drive to play hard and to win carried Nixon through four years on the four-man college debate team. They debated free trade versus protectionism and whether Allied war debts should be canceled and whether a free economy was superior to one managed by government. One year Frank Nixon lent the team his Packard for a 3,500-mile (5,600-km) debate tour of the Pacific Northwest.

In debating, Nixon grew familiar with many political issues and developed his public-speaking skills. Even in defeat, he tried to learn something. After one loss, the team manager, Kenn Ball, said, Nixon was extremely angry because he felt the team should have won. He was ready to stalk out of the room, but then he got himself under control and stopped to ask the debate judge what he had done wrong. The judge told him he had not clearly defined the issue involved. The next time, Nixon expressed his points more clearly.

All through college, he dated Ola Florence Welch, his girlfriend from high school. But by their senior year, they had both started dating other people. She found him intellectual and extremely interested in politics. But he seemed shy and lonely at times in spite of his success in campus politics and debate. "He didn't know how to mix," she said. "He would never double date. He had no real boy friends. And he didn't like my girl friends. He would stalk out of the room where they were, his head high."[12]

Then at one big dance, Nixon got angry with Ola and drove off alone, leaving her to call her parents to come and get her. The upshot was that Ola soon found another serious boyfriend.

In college politics, Nixon kept setting new goals. In May 1933, shortly after Harold died, he announced that he was running for president of the student body against a member of the Franklins, Dick Thomson. Nixon's chief campaign pledge was that if elected he would persuade the school's trustees to allow dances on campus for the first time. Thomson, meanwhile, pledged to work for the building of a new student union.

Nixon himself was an awkward dancer, and he rarely enjoyed parties, so it seemed like a strange promise for him to make. But he had a sense even then for what the voters wanted. "That campaign, as far as I see it, was merely the tremendous ability that Nixon had to see the situation and to take advantage of it," said Merton Wray, a fellow Whittier student.[13]

After winning the election, Nixon moved quickly to make good on his pledge. But would the touchy Quaker trustees yield?

"Think of the nerve of this lad," said Professor Paul Smith, "appearing before the august body, the Board of Trustees at Whittier College, in a plea of dancing on that campus, which the Quakers didn't look fondly upon at all. That was a rule from the time the college was founded. It took a lot of guts and nerve and crust, I think, to do that."[14]

The trustees gave in and began allowing monthly dances in the gym.

By the time he graduated with his B.A. in history, Nixon had succeeded in amazing many classmates with his good grades (he stood second in his class) and with his school activities. As a senior, the yearbook featured a separate article on him. But some fellow students thought his school spirit might be somewhat insincere. "I used to wonder if it was wholly genuine," said one classmate, "how much was simulated for the benefit of all present."[15]

Nixon still wanted to make good on his childhood dream of becoming a lawyer. He found out about twenty-five $250 scholarships available to Duke University in Durham, North Carolina, which had recently founded a new law school. His faculty adviser, an English professor, wrote a warm recommendation for him: "At Whittier, Richard Nixon displayed a rich sense of humor, human understanding, personal eloquence, and a marked ability to lead. He is intellectually honest, modest and youthfully enthusiastic. If he has any handicap, it is his lack of sophistication."[16]

The day that Nixon learned that he had won the scholarship, he drove to Ola Welch's house to tell her the good news. He was thrilled and excited in a way she'd never seen him before. "He wasn't just fun, he was absolutely joyous, abandoned—the only time I can recall seeing him like that. He had bought an old 1930 Ford and we rode around in the car and just celebrated."[17] It would be one of their last good times together, because she would soon marry someone else.

But Nixon was ready to open a new door to his life. He was headed to the faraway places he had dreamed of as a child. His life, till then almost entirely limited to California, and in particular Whittier, would now take him thousands of miles from home.

In Durham, the dynamic former student-body president and honor student suffered some culture shock. Except for photos, he had never seen the Duke campus before. "For someone accustomed to California architecture and a small college like Whittier, Duke was like a medieval cathedral town. There were spires and towers and stained glass everywhere," he later wrote.[18]

And the young man who had been the big fish in the little pond of Whittier faced serious competition. Over half his class belonged to the prestigious Phi Beta Kappa honor society. Nixon learned that of the twenty-five people who had won scholarships for their first year of law school, only twelve would win renewal, based on their grades. So if he wanted to stay in school and keep the precious $25 a month, he faced endless hours of study in the library.

He was on a tight budget. His father was lending him $35 a month, and he had a library job that made him another $30. So for the first few months of law school, Nixon moved into an abandoned toolshed, 8 feet by 12 feet (2.4 m by 3.7 m), in the woods near the campus. A maintenance man who found him there studying was shocked at the cardboard-lined hovel. He told Nixon he would freeze to death. "I'll manage all right if you don't run me out," Nixon said.

The sympathetic man decided, "This boy must want an education real bad."[19]

But Nixon was not just interested in saving money for college. At Christmas break, he and his brother Don, who was attending private school in North Carolina, went to New York City to shop. Together they bought their mother a special gift—her very first fur piece.

Later, Nixon lived with three friends, Lyman Brownfield, Bill Perdue, and Frederick Albrink, in another one-room shack about 2 miles (3.2 km) off campus. The building, which the friends nicknamed Whippoorwill Manor, had no bathroom.

Each morning, the roommates stuffed paper in a metal stove and dressed as the rapidly burning fire roared away. Nixon kept his razor in the library where he worked, and shaved each morning in the rest room. In the afternoons, he showered after playing handball in the gym. His breakfast was often a mere candy bar.

The rough schedule meant that many students didn't date while in school, and Nixon didn't either. His roommates nicknamed him "Gloomy Gus" because of his serious study habits.

In spite of the tough courses, Nixon kept his scholarship, but he always stood behind Perdue and Brownfield in the rankings.

One time, the dean was late in posting the grades. Growing restless, Nixon and his friends went to the dean's office after hours and one of them squeezed through a window over the door. Several versions of the story have been told, and in some of them, Nixon was the one who crawled into the room.

Once they gained access to the office, the friends looked at the grades and left. Nixon found that he had fallen below third place to a B-plus average, but by the time he graduated he had raised his grade.

Many people have speculated about whether this incident was a forerunner of the Watergate break-in that took place during Nixon's presidency. But his old friends said the incident was very innocent. "We found the files with the grades and looked at them ... didn't take any ... didn't change any," said Frederick Albrink.[20]

As law school neared an end, Nixon worried over where he would go next. He still yearned for a career in politics, although many of his friends thought him too serious and uptight to make a good politician. "It just never entered our minds that he would make a career in politics," Albrink said.[21]

Many law students were aiming for the top—prestigious posts with New York law firms. Over Christmas vacation, Nixon and two friends went to Manhattan for job interviews. But it was the Depression and Duke was a brand-new law school, and only one firm showed any interest in Nixon. Nixon disliked the New York City weather and prices.

One of Nixon's professors told him that if he was interested in politics, he should return to California to practice law. A little discouraged about the East Coast, Nixon decided to do so.

Before he left Durham, however, there was the excitement of graduation, and Nixon's parents, brother Edward, and grandmother Milhous drove out for the ceremonies in June 1937. "It was a proud day for them, made more so by the fact that on the day they arrived an announcement was made that I had finished third in my class," Nixon said.[22]

CHAPTER THREE

ON THE FIRST CAMPAIGN TRAIL

R E T U R N I N G to Whittier to practice law, Nixon joined the law firm of an old family friend, Tom Bewley.

Like many young people starting out, his early experiences were a little rocky. His first case involved a woman suing her uncle for repayment of a loan. The court ordered that a house belonging to the uncle be sold to repay the debt. But Nixon bungled the sale, and the woman ended up suing the law firm a year later for malpractice. She won a $4,800 verdict, but Bewley blamed himself, not Nixon, for what went wrong. "Any mistake in that case was made by me, not him," he said.[1]

Business was slow because of the Depression, but Bewley put Nixon to work on accident cases and tax work, which he enjoyed. He disliked the divorce cases he also handled. "At first I was surprised by some of the intimate matters people argued about, and equally surprised by the fact that they could calmly sit down and tell a stranger, even their lawyer, about them," he said.[2]

Gradually, business picked up and Nixon became a partner in the firm. On the side, he also invested in a small company, Citra-Frost, which hoped to sell juice from a bumper crop of southern California oranges on the East Coast. The investors in the firm hoped to freeze the juice before shipping it. Nixon, who served as president of the company, spent long hours after his days in the law office squeezing oranges himself and experimenting with packages—glass, metal, paper, cellophane. Nothing worked, and the first shipment of juice spoiled. The company soon folded, leaving behind some angry investors, who blamed Nixon. He also lost his own savings.

Just as he had been active in college, Nixon was a joiner in the community. He became the youngest member of the Whittier College Board of Trustees, and he joined the 20–30 Club, a group of young businessmen under thirty years old. He also served as president of Duke and Whittier alumni groups.

Somehow, he found time to act in plays with the local little-theater group. In early 1938, he tried out in a church Sunday-school room for a part in a play called *The Dark Tower*. Also trying out that night was a young, slender woman with red-gold hair. "I found I could not take my eyes away from her," he later wrote. ". . . It was a case of love at first sight."[3]

The woman was twenty-six-year-old Pat Ryan, a new teacher in the business department at Whittier High School. Nixon offered her a ride home, and on the way he asked her for a date. When she said she was too busy, he replied, "You shouldn't say that, because someday I am going to marry you!"[4]

Pat Ryan, born Thelma Catherine Ryan in 1912, in Ely, Nevada, had had the same kind of hardworking childhood background as Nixon. When she was just a toddler, her family moved to Artesia, California, where her father had an 11-acre (4.5-hectare) truck farm. She and her brothers had to help harvest potatoes, tomatoes, peppers, and cauliflower. Thelma Catherine grew up being called "Pat" by her father and later adopted Patricia as her name.

When Pat was fourteen, her forty-six-year-old mother, Kate, died of stomach cancer, leaving Pat to clean house, cook, and do laundry for her father and brothers plus go to high school. But Pat managed to do it all and still stay cheerful. She never allowed herself to feel tired or sick, she claimed. "As a youngster, life was sort of sad," she said. "So

I had to cheer everybody up. I learned to be that kind of person."[5]

Shortly after Pat graduated from high school, her father also died, a victim of tuberculosis. Anxious to see the world, she traveled to New York City and worked in a hospital that treated TB patients. By 1933, she was back in California to attend the University of Southern California while juggling several part-time jobs, everything from dishing out macaroni and cheese in the school cafeteria to playing bit parts in crowd scenes in movies.

After graduating in 1937, she took the teaching job in Whittier, where she was a hit with her students. "She was happy, enthusiastic, sprightly," said one of her students, Robert Pierpoint, who later became a correspondent for CBS. "Her disposition was sunny, not intermittently, but all the time."[6]

For once in his life, Nixon tried to sit back and relax, doing what Pat liked to do—ice skating, skiing, and swimming. He put his level-headed, no-nonsense approach to life aside and sent her poems and flowers and called her "Miss Vagabond" or "Irish Gypsy." She kept telling him she wasn't ready to get married, but she told her friends that she liked his drive. "He was going places and he always saw the possibilities," she said. She predicted, "He's going to be president someday."[7]

By the summer of 1939, they were dating seriously and soon Nixon proposed marriage. Finally, one March day in 1940, they drove from Whittier to San Clemente to sit on a cliff and watch the sunset. As the stars began glowing, she finally agreed to marry him. On May 1, a worker from the Nixon Market delivered a basket of flowers to Pat, who was grading papers after school. Inside was the diamond engagement ring they had picked out together. A few days later Nixon wrote her a letter: "Dear One, through the years, whatever happens I shall always be with you—loving you more every hour and attempting to let you feel that love in your heart and life."[8]

On June 21, 1940, they were married by the president of

Whittier College in a quiet ceremony with family members and friends at the Mission Inn, a Spanish-style hotel with turrets, arches, and colonnades, in Riverside. Pat wore a short, blue lace dress and rose-colored hat.

Afterward, the couple took off by car on a two-week honeymoon in Mexico, down the Pan American Highway. They took canned goods so they wouldn't have to eat in restaurants and spent only $178 on the entire trip.

Soon after the Nixons married, World War II had begun in Europe. In 1941, Nixon was offered a job in Washington, D.C., thanks to one of his Duke professors, and the couple moved there. For Nixon, it was a chance to see how government worked from close up, even though he had only a lowly $3,200-a-year job in tire rationing with the Office of Price Administration. He decided that there were many jobs that government just couldn't get done. "I learned respect for the thousands of hard-working government employees and an equal contempt for most of the political appointees at the top. I saw government overlapping and government empire-building at first hand," he said.[9]

After the Japanese bombed Peal Harbor, and the United States entered the war, many men about Nixon's age were being drafted for military service. But his government job meant he didn't have to go. Most men in his family had gotten deferments because they were Quaker pacifists who did not believe in war. But Nixon enlisted in the Navy, even though he knew his mother thought he was violating Quaker principles. "The problem with Quaker pacifism, it seemed to me, was that it could only work if one were fighting a civilized, compassionate enemy," he said. "In the face of Hitler and Tojo, pacifism not only failed to stop violence—it actually played into the hands of a barbarous foe."[10]

Because of his interest in politics, being loyal to his country and serving in the armed forces during wartime also seemed like a political necessity.

Nixon was commissioned as a lieutenant and assigned to the South Pacific Combat Air Transport Command, nicknamed SCAT, on the island of New Caledonia. Although heavy fighting swept through the South Pacific, his assignment was far from the boom of the big guns and dangers of the battlefield. His unit unloaded supplies from cargo and transport planes and reloaded them with the wounded. As American fighting forces moved north through the South Pacific, Nixon's group moved to Bougainville in the Solomon Islands and then to Green Island. "I didn't get hit or hit anyone," he later said. "All I got was a case of fungus."[11]

But the Navy introduced Nixon to experiences largely foreign to him. He learned to like coffee and cigars; he drank whiskey and played poker. Although he later contended that reports of his poker prowess were greatly exaggerated, he admitted, "I found playing poker instructive as well as entertaining and profitable."[12]

Nixon and his friends played for hours during the long stretches between the landings of planes. Fellow officer Lester Wroble said he doubted that Nixon ever lost a cent. "He had a passion for analysis; he always played it cautious—close to the belt, and there was never a time when he didn't know exactly what he was doing."[13]

Although some pots in games ran as high as $1,000, most of the time Nixon won from about $30 to $60 a day. By war's end, his friends estimated that he might have saved between $3,500 and $10,000 from his winnings.

Besides earning a reputation as a whiz at poker, Nixon also won the respect and friendship of the enlisted men who served under him and often called him "Nick." Often there was intense pressure when dozens of planes touched down at once. Only the enlisted men were required to do loading and unloading, but Nixon took off his shirt and pitched in until the job was done.

On Green Island, he opened "Nixon's Snack Shack," where hungry pilots and crews got free coffee, sandwiches, and juices—food that Nixon had scrounged from other units with more supplies than his. Occasionally, he doled out cupfuls of whiskey. "If you ever saw Henry Fonda in *Mr. Roberts,* you have a pretty good idea of what Nick was like," said one fellow officer.[14]

In July 1944, Nixon returned to the United States and was assigned to the East Coast where he worked on Navy contracts with aircraft companies. Soon he was ready to leave the service. He and Pat, who was pregnant with their first child, planned to return to Whittier so he could pick up his law practice again.

But in the fall of 1945, while he was still in the East, Nixon received a letter that led to a more dramatic turn in his career. Herman Perry, an influential Whittier banker, wondered if Nixon was interested in running for Congress in 1946 as a Republican facing Jerry Voorhis, the Democratic incumbent in the Twelfth Congressional District, which included Whittier.

Perry represented a group of Republicans who disliked Democratic presidents Franklin Delano Roosevelt and Harry Truman and FDR's New Deal policies. The group, the Committee of One Hundred, paid for Nixon and Pat to fly out briefly to California. Still in a Navy uniform, Nixon made a speech to some seventy Committee members, as did five other prospective candidates. Nixon told the group that returning veterans did not want government handouts. They wanted respectable jobs in private industry and a chance to start their own businesses. "I will be prepared," he said, "to put on an aggressive and vigorous campaign on a platform of practical liberalism and with your help I feel very strongly that the present incumbent can be defeated."[15]

Nixon outshone the other candidates and received sixty-three votes of those present. He was jubilant when he got the call telling him the news and began reading up on his opponent and interviewing Republicans in Congress about Voorhis.

From the start, he knew Voorhis was a formidable and popular foe even though the district was largely Republican. The congressman, seeking his sixth term, was the son of a millionaire but had given up his father's wealth to work at several humble jobs. He had also used some of his family's money to build an orphanage.

Early in his career, Voorhis had been a Socialist but later

became a Democrat. In his first election, he was carried into office on the coattails of the popular Franklin Roosevelt. As the years passed, Voorhis became a strong opponent of Communism and sponsored the Voorhis Act, a law requiring any organization controlled by a foreign power to register with the Department of Justice. Communists had bitterly opposed this bill.

Soon Nixon and Pat moved into a small house in Whittier and began a barebones campaign, largely financed out of his own pocket. Friends and family donated office furniture and helped him campaign, but his main office staff was Pat. She worked until a few days before their first daughter, Patricia, nicknamed "Tricia," was born on February 21. By mid-March, she was back on the job, typing campaign literature, stuffing envelopes, and handing out brochures. Meanwhile, Nixon worked twenty hours a day, making and writing speeches, visiting service clubs, and holding coffee hours in friendly homes.

Despite the Nixons' backbreaking work, no one gave Nixon much chance. In the primary, in which candidates could register for both the Democratic and Republican nominations, Voorhis beat Nixon by 7,500 votes in the combined total.

Nixon made the usual Republican promises to fight big government and laws that were tough on small-business people. But he soon picked a new campaign issue: a claim that Jerry Voorhis was sympathetic to Communism. "I expected a tough campaign in 1946," Voorhis later said. ". . . I did not expect my loyalty to America's constitutional government to be attacked."[16]

Voorhis and many others believed that Nixon had fallen under the influence of Murray Chotiner, a Beverly Hills public relations man, who had worked for several big-name California politicians. Chotiner was known for hard-hitting, sometimes shady, campaigns. He did give some advice to Nixon, but for the most part, Nixon made his own campaign decisions.

In speech after speech that summer, Nixon claimed that

Voorhis had a voting record tainted by Socialism and Communism. He also contended that Voorhis had been endorsed by the CIO union's political action committee, known as CIO-PAC, which had a number of Communists as leaders. In fact the group had refused to endorse Voorhis in 1946, although it had done so in 1944. Voorhis denied Nixon's charges and produced an editorial from the Communist newspaper *People's World* in which he was soundly denounced.

Then in September the two candidates debated in front of an independent voters' group in South Pasadena. Once again, the question of the endorsement by the political action committee came up, and Nixon was prepared. The young challenger pulled out of his pocket a copy of a bulletin from another liberal group, the National Citizens Political Action Committee, or NCPAC, recommending that Voorhis be endorsed. Voorhis was stunned. The two groups were actually different organizations, and he tried to explain that to the audience.

In response Nixon read a list of the names of people who belonged to both groups. The committees might have different names, but they amounted to the same thing, he said. "Considering the close ties between the two PACS, I thought that the question of which PAC had endorsed him was a distinction without difference," Nixon later wrote in his memoirs.[17]

At the debate and for several days, Voorhis stumbled again and again as he tried to respond. Nixon then challenged Voorhis to four more debates, and the congressman felt compelled to agree to them. The debates drew huge crowds and flocks of reporters. At each one, cheering sections yelled and clapped for their favorite candidate. For the last debate, more than 1,000 people jammed the Monrovia High School gym in San Gabriel and loudspeakers boomed the voices of the candidates to crowds standing outside.

Again and again, Nixon hammered away on the endorsement issue and charged that Voorhis had done little in Congress. Voorhis responded weakly.

In an October campaign ad, Nixon claimed that Voorhis

had introduced 132 bills in Congress in four years, and that only one ever passed. That one bill, Nixon said, was a law transferring activities concerning rabbits from one federal department to another. On the defensive again, Voorhis tried to explain that he had been involved in getting many bills passed but that few congressmen actually had bills named for them.

Momentum had swung to Nixon, and contributions poured in for his campaign. He spent heavily for advertising and brochures and reimbursed himself for the savings he spent on his race.

On Election Day, Nixon won a smashing victory at the polls and received 65,586 votes to Voorhis's 49,994. The Nixons were thrilled. "Nothing could equal the excitement and jubilation of winning the first campaign," he later said.[18]

But Nixon had also lost something in the campaign, the innocence and squeaky-clean image that many people had seen in him until then. During the Voorhis campaign, where was the compassionate brother who had been shocked and stunned by the deaths of Harold and Arthur Nixon? Where was the Quaker boy who had played piano in church? Where was the hardworking youth who had pleaded with his parents not to turn a shoplifter over to the police?

In his first campaign for office, Nixon had also split voters into groups of Nixon-haters and Nixon-lovers. No one in the Twelfth District was neutral on the question of his character; everyone had an opinion. Some years later, when the city council of Whittier proposed naming a new street after him, a group blocked the plan; and some Whittier College students protested when he came to speak at a commencement in 1954.

For the rest of his life, Nixon tried to explain that first campaign. Communism wasn't really the main issue in 1946, he contended in his memoirs. People were upset about price controls, shortages of goods, strikes, and government mismanagement, he insisted. "Although Voorhis was a hardworking and generally respected congressman, he was not really in tune with the voters of the district," he said.[19]

Nixon also argued, "If some of my rhetoric seems overstated now, it was nonetheless in keeping with the approach that seasoned Republican politicians were using that year."[20]

Nixon's daughter Julie Nixon Eisenhower said the same thing in a biography of her mother. The central campaign issue, she said, was really New Deal politics and Voorhis's place in Washington. Regarding the political-action-committee charges, she said, not until her father made the PAC endorsement an issue did Voorhis contact PAC national headquarters in New York and ask that its endorsement be withdrawn.

The fact was, however, that Nixon had used anti-Communism as a campaign issue long before anyone else tried to do so.

CHAPTER FOUR

NIXON VERSUS ALGER HISS

S O O N after the election, the Nixons drove the 3,000 miles (4,800 km) to Washington, D.C., with their suitcases and pots and kettles jammed in their Ford. They found postwar Washington packed with people scrambling for housing. After months in a motel, they found a two-bedroom duplex in Park Fairfax, Virginia.

The couple felt awkward and uncomfortable for the first few months; they were Westerners unaccustomed to the fast-paced, high-style life of the nation's movers and shakers. Once that first year, a prominent congressman invited the Nixons to a party where dress was supposed to be "informal." So Pat wore a cocktail dress and Nixon wore a blue suit. They arrived to find everyone else in tuxedoes with black ties or in long evening gowns. "Formal" meant tuxedoes with *white* ties.

But Nixon soon befriended other young freshmen Republican congressmen, many assigned as he was to "the attic"— the fifth floor of the House Office Building. One of Nixon's Democratic acquaintances was a young congressman from Massachusetts, also a freshman in the Eightieth Congress— John F. Kennedy. Although the two often voted differently on bills, Nixon contended that there was no bitterness between them. "He was shy, and that sometimes made him appear aloof. But it was the shyness born of an instinct that guarded privacy and concealed emotions. I understood these qualities because I shared them," Nixon later wrote.[1]

Despite his inexperience, Nixon was appointed to the important Education and Labor Committee, where he worked for passage of the Taft-Hartley Bill, which would limit the power of labor unions. When the bill passed, President Harry Truman, a Democrat, vetoed it, but Congress overrode his veto.

Nixon attracted even more attention because of another committee assignment, on the often controversial House Committee on Un-American Activities, often referred to as HUAC.

The committee was investigating activities of the Communist Party in the United States, and many people felt that it had become a judge and jury that trampled on the rights of so-called Communists. After all, it was not illegal to simply *be* a Communist.

But many Americans were worried about Communism. They were frightened by the Soviet influence in Europe and the rise of Socialist political groups in European countries. They also feared that the Russians might somehow steal America's atom-bomb secrets. Even President Truman announced that he was prepared to intervene in nations where the Communists might try to subjugate free people.

In July 1947, Nixon was chosen to go with a special committee, headed by Congressman Christian Herter of Massachusetts, to study the rise of Communist political groups in Europe. The committee was trying to determine whether Congress should support a proposal by Secretary of State George Marshall to provide billions of dollars in aid to Western Europe as a way of keeping Communist groups at bay. Nixon was the youngest congressman chosen to go.

Many of Nixon's supporters in California opposed the Marshall Plan. After all, the Democrats had proposed it, and California Republicans viewed it as a giant giveaway of taxpayers' money. But Nixon was quickly persuaded that only the Marshall Plan could help keep war-torn Europe from falling into the hands of anarchists and revolutionaries. "Without American aid, millions would starve or die of diseases caused by malnutrition before the winter was over," Nixon said.[2]

Nixon felt he had to vote his conscience. He wrote newspaper columns for California papers that described what he had seen and why the aid was needed to keep Europe free of Communism. As soon as he could, he also went home to California to tour for a month and give speeches on the Marshall Plan.

In the fall of 1947, Nixon was only slightly involved in the investigation that HUAC was conducting into Communist infiltration of Hollywood. Producers, directors, writers, and actors were called in and asked to tell if they had ever belonged to the Communist Party and to give names of fellow Communists. Somehow Nixon stayed clear of the fighting and name-calling.

But he did work with a Republican senator, Karl Mundt of South Dakota, on a bill to require registration of Communist Party members. The point of the bill was not to outlaw the party and drive it underground, as some congressmen wanted, but to expose its activities to public view. That was the best way, Nixon believed, to control Communist activities in the United States.

The bill passed the House of Representatives by a huge margin in 1948, but by the time it reached the Senate, liberals throughout the country were battling the bill. It never got out of committee in the Senate, although some of its provisions later became law as part of the McCarran Act of 1950.

Was there ever any real danger that Communists were going to overthrow the government of the United States? Looking back on that time, it seems unlikely. Many who had belonged to the Communist Party in the 1930s and 1940s had dropped out when they learned about the reign of terror by Joseph Stalin in the Soviet Union and the Soviet aggression in Eastern Europe. The Communist Party was in disarray, often split among different factions.

But many Republicans in the late 1940s were determined to prove that the Democrats, who had controlled the presidency and Congress for so long, had allowed many Communist sympathizers to hold powerful government jobs. Involvement in one of these cases presented Nixon with what he called the first major crisis of his political career.

It all began on August 3, 1948, when HUAC heard the testimony of Whittaker Chambers, a Communist who later left the party and became a senior editor for *Time* magazine. The pudgy and sloppy Chambers made a poor first impression on Nixon. "His clothes were unpressed. His shirt collar was curled up over his jacket. He spoke in a rather bored monotone," Nixon said.[3]

But his half-mumbled words quickly caught Nixon's attention. Chambers said he had joined the Communist Party in 1924 because he believed it could save the world and that he left in 1939 after deciding that the party advocated totalitarian government. Then he named several government officials who he alleged belonged to his underground Communist cell. One was a former State Department official, Alger Hiss, who had once served as temporary secretary general of the United Nations. Later Hiss left government to become president of a large private foundation, the Carnegie Endowment.

Newspaper headlines the next day bannered Chambers's charges, and Hiss demanded a chance to respond. When the forty-three-year-old Hiss testified, the committee faced a handsome, polished, and witty man who was thoroughly in command of himself. A member of a prestigious Eastern family, he had graduated from Johns Hopkins University and Harvard Law School and had held several important government jobs.

Hiss not only denied any link to the Communist Party, but he also denied ever having heard the name Whittaker Chambers. Looking at a photo of Chambers, he would not swear that he had never met the man, but he indicated that Chambers was a stranger to him. "Without actually saying it, he left the clear impression that he was the innocent victim of a terrible case of mistaken identity," Nixon said.[4]

But the congressman from Whittier was not impressed. Nixon felt that when people lied, they often overstated their case, and that is what he felt Hiss had done.

As the hearing closed, some congressmen and many spectators crowded around Hiss to shake his hand; reporters on hand were convinced the committee had blundered. How could the committee ever get away with this? one reporter asked Nixon.

In fact, the other committee members were ready to drop the matter, but Nixon wanted to press on. Although they might not prove that Hiss was a Communist, he said, they might prove that the two men did know each other. If Hiss had lied about Chambers, he might be lying about the Communist Party. Because of the important jobs Hiss had held, Nixon said, it was vital to investigate further. The committee agreed to call Chambers in for a private meeting, and Nixon began combing the testimony of the two men.

Nixon believed he was at an important crossroads, about to face a turning point in his life. His political future was at stake. The Washington press was in an uproar and contended that the committee had sullied an innocent man by allowing Chambers to testify. Even President Truman condemned the hearings.

When Chambers reappeared at a closed session, he gave many details about Hiss's life and family that at first sounded convincing to Nixon. But later Nixon had doubts. Perhaps Chambers had carefully studied Hiss's life and then concocted the whole complex story. The committee investigators, headed by Robert Stripling, began visiting old friends and neighbors of the two men. They also hoped to find documents to verify Chambers's story, such as his claim that Hiss once gave him a 1929 Ford Roadster, even though the Communist Party had objected that it might create a link between the two men. So instead, Chambers said, Hiss had to sign the car over to another man.

Still troubled, Nixon wanted to talk to Chambers one-on-one. He made the first of several two-hour car trips to Chambers's farm in Westminster, Maryland, to interview the witness privately. They sat in rocking chairs on the front porch overlooking rolling hills while Nixon told Chambers what all of Washington was saying, that Chambers must have some grudge against Hiss. "Certainly I wouldn't have a motive which would involve destroying my own career," Chambers said.[5]

Nixon was impressed with Chambers's sincerity and with his worries over what the affair might do to his wife and children.

Soon committee members met with Hiss privately, and this time many believed that Hiss was evading their questions and changing his testimony. He said that Chambers's photo did seem familiar. Perhaps Chambers was the magazine writer to whom he had once subleased an apartment. The man's name, he claimed, was George Crosley. Crosley had failed to pay all the rent but had given Hiss a Persian carpet for part of his debt, Hiss said.

It was arranged for Hiss and Chambers to meet in a suite at a New York City hotel. Hiss and committee members were seated at chairs next to a table when Chambers walked into the living room through the bedroom door. Hatred seemed to radiate from Hiss to Chambers, Nixon said.

Previously, Hiss had said that the man he called Crosley had very bad teeth. Now he asked that Chambers open his mouth so he could look at his teeth. "Hiss's hand was not more than six inches [15 cm] from Chambers's mouth, and at that moment I wondered whether Chambers was tempted to bite his finger," Nixon said.[6]

Finally, Hiss identified Chambers as the man he called George Crosley. But he still claimed that he had not known that Chambers/Crosley was a Communist.

All this time Nixon was working longer hours than ever before in his life—eighteen to twenty hours a day. His family scarcely saw him, and when they did he was tense and irritable. "I lost interest in eating and skipped meals without even being aware of it. Getting to sleep became more and more difficult."[7] Nixon's second daughter, Julie, had been born on July 5, but because of the Hiss case, the family had to postpone plans to get out of the sticky Washington summer with the new baby.

Finally, the big day came, the public confrontation between Hiss and Chambers, where Nixon believed the committee would prove itself. All the East Coast liberals and intellectuals who had backed Hiss, he believed, would have to admit they had been wrong.

The open meeting was held in a Washington, D.C., hearing room jammed with reporters and TV cameras. Hiss talked about his career and his distinguished friends. He insisted that conflicts between his story and that of Chambers made no difference—the only real question was whether he had been a Communist.

But the real bombshell for Hiss was that the committee had found the paperwork on the car given to Chambers. Hiss had admitted giving the car to the man he called Crosley, but the papers showed that Hiss signed the car over to a man who was a Communist organizer.

For five hours, under hot television lights, committee members grilled Hiss. At the end, Nixon felt relieved. Although Hiss still had many supporters, many of Nixon's critics admitted they had made a mistake. The committee's role in the Hiss case seemed over. Hiss filed suit against Chambers for libel, but it looked as if the Justice Department might indict Hiss for perjury, or lying to Congress.

Nixon was reelected easily to a second four-year term in November. It was a rewarding triumph, but Democratic president Truman also won reelection.

After the election, Nixon and Pat made plans for a December cruise that would pass through the Panama Canal, their first vacation in three years. But the day before they were supposed to sail, Nixon read an item in the Washington papers that stunned him. The Justice Department was thinking of indicting Chambers instead of Hiss. Chambers had gotten into trouble during pretrial testimony in the libel case by producing State Department documents that he said Hiss gave him during the 1930s to pass to the Communist Party for possible use by the Soviet Union.

It looked like espionage to the Justice Department lawyers, and they decided that Chambers could be indicted for lying to the committee when he said he had never been a spy. No account seemed to be taken of the possibility that Hiss might have stolen the documents, and the Justice Department seemed to be inclined to keep them under wraps, out of the public eye.

Nixon was angry at the Justice Department for what he believed was a cover-up and an attempt to save the Truman administration from embarrassment, but he was also upset with Chambers for not telling him about the documents. Nixon's advisers, including investigator Robert Stripling, urged him not to leave town. They wanted to serve an immediate subpoena on Chambers to get more documents that could nail Hiss for espionage. But although Nixon was willing to order the subpoena, he refused to cancel his vacation. But once the Nixons set sail, Stripling kept sending Nixon telegrams urging him to return: SECOND BOMBSHELL OBTAINED BY SUBPOENA 1 A.M. FRIDAY. CASE CLINCHED. INFORMATION AMAZING.[8]

The relaxing vacation ended after only a few days. Nixon arranged for a Coast Guard seaplane to fly out to the ship to pick him up and take him back to Miami while Pat Nixon was left behind. Hordes of reporters greeted him in Miami and demanded a comment. Flashbulbs popped as photographers snapped front-page photos of Nixon leaving the plane.

Back in Washington, the committee investigators told him how Chambers had led them to a frosty pumpkin patch on his farm. There he popped the top off a hollowed-out pumpkin and pulled out three cylinders of microfilm. The developed film revealed what came to be called "the pumpkin papers"—hundreds of pages of government documents that Hiss had allegedly given to Chambers. Chambers had hidden the film in the pumpkin in case any unsympathetic federal officials searched his house.

Although many complained that the documents involved were not important ones, they still suggested that Hiss, a friend and adviser to presidents and secretaries of state, had been deeply involved in the Communist Party.

The federal government was under pressure to try Hiss for some sort of crime. The statute of limitations made it impossible to indict him for spying, but he was indicted for perjury—for lying when he said he had not taken documents from the State Department, and for lying when he said he had not seen Chambers after a certain date in 1937. He was eventually found guilty, in 1950, and served about four years in prison.

The question of Hiss's guilt or innocence has been widely debated for years. Hiss continued to insist he was innocent. Even some of those who felt he must have been a Communist believed that he had never done anything really wrong. Needless to say, Nixon became a hotly debated political figure on the national stage. Undoubtedly, Nixon said, the Hiss case put him on the road to running for vice president. But he added, "It also turned me from a relatively popular young congressman, enjoying a good but limited press, into one of the most controversial figures in Washington, bitterly opposed by the most respected and influential liberal journalists and opinion leaders of the time."[9]

CHAPTER FIVE

NEW RACES TO WIN

W I T H his new national image, Nixon was ready to move ahead. He decided to run for the Senate in a 1950 race against the incumbent Democrat, Sheridan Downey. But he was surprised to find that the business people who had backed him against Jerry Voorhis were upset. They believed he had a strong seat in the House and would be risking it foolishly by running for a new office that few felt he could win.

Although he lacked their wholehearted support, Nixon announced his candidacy on November 3, 1949.

Very quickly, it turned out that his main opponent would not be Downey but a congresswoman, Helen Gahagan Douglas, who opposed Downey for the Democratic nomination. Douglas was a former actress and the wife of actor Melvyn Douglas. She was much more of a liberal than Downey and had worked hard for housing for the poor and against HUAC. Two months before the primary, Downey withdrew and was succeeded by Manchester Boddy, publisher of the Los Angeles *Daily News.* Boddy was a conservative and waged a bitter campaign against Douglas. He implied that she had helped the Communists by voting against aid to Greece and Turkey.

Things could not have worked out better for Nixon. While the two Democrats scratched and clawed each other, he stood on the sidelines. He also benefited when Douglas eventually won the Democratic nomination. Manchester Boddy's political ideas were too much like Nixon's. Facing Douglas gave Nixon more of a chance to use his image as a conservative fighter against Communism.

During the campaign, Pat and Dick Nixon traveled thousands and thousands of miles in a secondhand wood-paneled Mercury station wagon with NIXON FOR SENATE signs tacked on the sides. When they stopped in small towns, a sound system on top of the car announced that the candidate had arrived. They then lowered the tailgate so Nixon could stand on it and speak.

Until then many Americans had believed that the Communist threat was exaggerated, but events in 1949 and 1950 seemed to back up many of Nixon's charges and predictions. In the fall of 1949, Mao Tse-tung and the Communist Chinese took over the government of China and the Russians successfully tested their first atomic bomb. In 1950, several Americans went on trial for supposedly passing atomic secrets to the Soviets.

Shortly after the June 7 primary when Nixon and Douglas were chosen to represent their parties, the Communist North Koreans invaded South Korea, an event which also boosted Nixon's chances. Suddenly, all his speeches about Communism seemed believable.

As the race heated up, charges flew back and forth. Nixon's campaign was being run by Murray Chotiner, the wily campaigner who had helped make William Knowland a Republican senator from California and Earl Warren the governor of California. Just as in the Voorhis campaign, Nixon accused his Democratic opponent of being a Communist sympathizer. But Douglas threw plenty of dirt at Nixon as well, a fact that many people do not remember.

Strangely enough, a Douglas campaign mail piece accused Nixon of voting against aid to Korea. One of her most famous campaign flyers became known as the "yellow sheet" and said: "THE BIG LIE! Hitler invented it. Stalin perfected it. Nixon uses it. . . . YOU pick the Congressman the Kremlin loves!"[1] But besides accusing him of aiding the Communists, she also charged that Nixon was a fascist and an anti-Semite because of an endorsement he received from a racist agitator, Gerald L. K. Smith.

Nixon denounced Smith and put out a "pink sheet" of his own claiming that Douglas had voted 354 times the same way as a congressman who was often accused of being a Communist sympathizer. Nixon failed to mention that he had voted with the same congressman 112 times.

Chotiner started calling Douglas "the Pink Lady," a term he picked up from a local newspaper. She, in turn, came up with the nickname "Tricky Dick" for Nixon, a label that his critics threw at him for the rest of his life. Somehow though, Nixon succeeded in making his charges about Douglas stick tighter than those she used on him.

The mudslinging continued right up until election day. Nixon was pessimistic about his chances, but he won the election by a 680,000-vote margin. That night, the Nixons went from one victory party to another, and whenever Nixon found a piano handy, he sat down to play "Happy Days Are Here Again."

In spite of his fierce and sometimes questionable tactics, Nixon believed that the Douglas campaign had been far more vicious than his. She waged a campaign, he later said, "that would not be equaled for stridency, ineptness, or self-righteousness until George McGovern's presidential campaign twenty-two years later."[2]

Nixon's victory and the strong showing he soon made in the Senate captured the attention of supporters of Dwight Eisenhower, the Army general who led Allied forces to victory in Europe against Hitler during World War II. Eisenhower had announced in January 1952 that he would run for the presidency as the Republican candidate.

The Eisenhower forces liked Nixon's reputation as an anti-Communist. But surprisingly enough, Nixon was also viewed as something of a moderate because he had supported giving postwar aid to Europe through the Marshall Plan. Despite the strong language used in his campaigns, Nixon also held off from throwing unsubstantiated charges at other politicians once he was in the Senate. He was viewed as someone with support from both conservatives and liberals in the Republican Party.

Nixon liked Eisenhower as well. He believed that Eisenhower, who was enormously popular with the general public, was the only Republican with a chance of becoming president. Old-time Republicans, known as the Old Guard, felt differently and favored Ohio senator Robert Taft. They believed Eisenhower was too liberal in his political views.

Early in 1952, Taft went to Nixon and asked for his support at the Republican National Convention. "It was with a great deal of sadness that I told him I personally felt that international affairs would be more important for the next President and that I had concluded Eisenhower was the best qualified in that area," Nixon later said.[3] Taft graciously told Nixon he was disappointed but respected his decision.

Over the next few months, Nixon made many speeches attacking the Democrats and President Truman. He urged election of a Republican as president without actually naming whom he wanted, but behind the scenes he worked for Eisenhower.

In May, Eisenhower's inner circle of advisers invited him to Washington, where he joined them to discuss foreign and national issues with Nixon for several hours. "Nothing was said about the vice presidency," Nixon said, "but it was clear that they were trying to get to know me better and to size me up."[4]

Although Nixon denied having serious designs on the vice presidency, his political maneuvering spoke more loudly than his words.

Clearly, the scene was shaping up for a huge battle among the candidates at the Republican National Convention in Chicago in July 1952. The governor of California, Earl Warren, had won that state's primary, and Nixon was pledged to vote for him, as were other state delegates. But just before the convention, Nixon sent 23,000 questionnaires to California voters asking them who they thought would be the strongest nominee. Most said it was Eisenhower. The Warren forces were furious when they heard about this mini-poll. Warren was hoping for a deadlock between Taft and Eisenhower, in which case he might swoop in to take the nomination. Warren's supporters charged that Nixon was trying to woo California delegates for Eisenhower in return for the vice presidency.

At the convention, a fight broke out over which candidate's delegates, Taft's, or Eisenhower's, should be seated from the states of Georgia and Texas. California's role was crucial in settling this dispute. If its delegates supported the Taft delegates, Taft would win the nomination. If they went for the Eisenhower delegates, Eisenhower would win. And if they split, as Governor Warren wanted, Warren might have his chance for the nomination.

On a train carrying the California delegates to the convention, Nixon went from delegate to delegate lobbying for Eisenhower's delegation from the South. The Warren forces were angry and wanted to put Nixon off the train. But in the end, Nixon won out. The California delegation went 62 to 8 for what the Eisenhower forces called the Fair Play amendment, a measure that seated their Southern delegation.

By then, the Chicago papers were predicting that Nixon would get the vice-presidential nod if Eisenhower was the party's choice, and Nixon began to believe it himself. One person remained to be convinced, Pat Nixon. One night she came back to her hotel room to find Nixon, upbeat and excited about the chance to run for vice president. Pat Nixon argued against the idea. "My mother was wary—and realistic," Julie Nixon Eisenhower wrote later. "She resisted being swept away by the surface glamour of the idea."[5]

They had just finished the grueling Senate campaign that had taken Pat Nixon away from her young daughters for many long hours. Since his election as senator, Nixon practically lived at the Capitol, often spending the night sleeping on the couch in his office. For several hours, Pat argued against this new idea. She was a good campaigner, but she yearned to keep what private life she had left.

At 4:00 A.M., Nixon called Murray Chotiner into the room to get his opinion. "There comes a point," Chotiner said, "when you have to go up or go out." Pat finally surrendered. "I guess I can make it through another campaign," she said. But she still hoped that the vice-presidential nomination might fall through.[6]

The next day, Eisenhower was nominated for president quickly and easily on the first ballot, but not without leaving hard feelings behind among the Taft and Warren forces. Nixon returned to his hotel room for a nap, while the Eisenhower people convened to pick a vice president.

Nixon had just drifted off to sleep when the phone rang. An Eisenhower aide was calling to tell him that he had been chosen as the nominee. Nixon jumped out of bed and rode via limousine with a police escort to Eisenhower's hotel. In a very serious and formal conversation, Eisenhower asked him if he would be his running mate and Nixon accepted. Eisenhower made it clear that he intended to take a lofty above-politics position during the campaign while Nixon had to lead the attack against the Democrats, their presidential nominee, Illinois governor Adlai Stevenson, and his running mate, John Sparkman. But Nixon would also have to reach out to the Taft delegates who were hurt and angry that their candidate had lost.

The two candidates then went to the convention hall, and at 6:33 P.M. Nixon became the vice-presidential nominee. Nixon and his wife went up to the rostrum while cheers and applause from thousands thundered through the hall. "I felt exhilarated—almost heady—as I looked out across the moving, shifting mass that filled the convention floor and galleries," Nixon said.[7]

Several weeks later, the serious campaigning began. Eisenhower boarded a special train, the *Look Ahead, Neighbor Special,* to tour the Midwest. Meanwhile, Nixon left Pomona, California, on a train called the *Nixon Special.* Standing at the back of a car, he pledged to clean up Washington and fight the corruption that he said had tainted Truman's administration.

It was a moment to savor and remember. In less than three years, Nixon had gone from the House of Representatives to become the nominee for the second highest office in the nation. He had played a major role in the nomination of Dwight Eisenhower as president. All this, and he was only thirty-nine years old. Not bad for the boy who had once sorted vegetables for his father's grocery store and had to turn down a Harvard scholarship because he didn't have enough money.

But a major roadblock lay just around the bend for the *Nixon Special,* one that Nixon would later view as one of the major crises in his life, and one that came close to derailing his hopes of becoming vice president.

A COCKER SPANIEL AND A CLOTH COAT

I T seemed trivial and insignificant in the beginning. A few days before the *Nixon Special* chugged off, a newspaper columnist asked him about a fund set up by some California businessmen for Nixon. Supporters of Earl Warren, disgruntled at Nixon, had begun spreading rumors about the fund at the Republican Convention. Some claimed that Nixon was getting a supplementary salary of $20,000 a year out of the fund.

The reporter's question didn't upset Nixon at first. He admitted that a fund had been arranged to pay for his trips back and forth between California and Washington and for personal and political messages that he could not send for free as part of his mailing privileges as a senator. The total he had received in two years was $18,235. A special trustee handled the fund, and no one was allowed to contribute more than $500 to it. No companies could donate money, he explained, only private individuals. "All expenditures were for mailing, travel and other political activities. Not a cent was used for solely personal purposes," Nixon said.[1]

Although it seemed as if Nixon had set up the fund very carefully and properly, the big question in the minds of the press was whether the contributors had received special favors in return for their gifts. And although Nixon wasn't using the money to buy himself cars and other luxuries, the money donated for his trips to his home district was money he didn't have to take out of his own pocket.

Nixon wasn't worried. Clearly there was nothing illegal about the fund, he thought. His advisers agreed with him. Murray Chotiner told him the whole story was a ridiculous tempest in a teapot.

His campaign train steamed off from Pomona, California, on September 18 with a scent of victory in the air. All the polls showed that the Eisenhower-Nixon ticket was far ahead of Stevenson-Sparkman, and Nixon believed that this would be an easy campaign compared to the bitter, mudslinging races he had battled through in the past.

But that day, newspaper headlines blared out statements like this: SECRET RICH MEN'S TRUST FUND KEEPS NIXON IN STYLE FAR BEYOND HIS SALARY.[2] As the storm brewed into a hurricane, Nixon continued his whistlestop tour—to Bakersfield, Tulare, Fresno, Stockton, and Sacramento in California and then on to Oregon and Washington State. But at each train stop, more and more reporters climbed aboard and demanded to know about the fund. Hecklers at his train stops yelled at him: "Tell us about the $18,000!"[3]

Meanwhile, the fund story was rocking Washington, D.C. The Republican National Committee was deluged by phone calls, and many Republicans seemed to feel that Nixon might have to resign his nomination. The Democrats chimed in, urging Nixon to quit and to stop making charges about how unethical the Truman administration had been. But through it all, Adlai Stevenson seemed strangely silent.

Aboard the train, it was difficult for the Nixon staff to make phone calls and get new information about the growing crisis, so at first Nixon believed that the fund story was nothing more than tough campaign tactics as usual. He decided to release the list of all his contributors so that everyone could see they were not millionaires. But he was worried because he hadn't heard from General Eisenhower for two days after the newspaper stories began to break. At first Eisenhower's staff had withheld the news of the fund from the general. When Eisenhower finally was told, he issued a statement that "the facts will show that Nixon would not compromise with what is right."[4]

Then a major blow fell. Nixon learned that two major East Coast newspapers had published editorials calling for Nixon to resign. One of them, the New York *Herald Tribune,* was a strongly Republican paper with close ties to General Eisenhower, so Nixon began to believe that perhaps Eisenhower himself wanted him to quit. Still he heard no direct message from the general. He soon learned that the Eisenhower train was in an uproar. Half of the general's advisers believed that Nixon should resign; half thought he should stick it out.

Nixon felt like a prisoner aboard the campaign train. He was unable to talk to Eisenhower directly, unable to do more than face hostile reporters.

Finally, after a long meeting with his staff, Nixon told Pat about the editorial and said he was finished and had better resign. But Pat was furious. "If you do, Eisenhower will lose," she said. "He can put you off the ticket if he wants to, but if you, in the face of attack, do not fight back but simply crawl away, you will destroy yourself. Your life will be marred forever and the same will be true of your family, and particularly, your daughters."[5]

Finally the train arrived in Portland, and the Nixons disembarked for a hotel. But the scene was ugly: an angry crowd threw pennies into their car and pushed and jostled them on the sidewalk. But a plan was beginning to form on the Nixon side. Nixon's chief adviser, Chotiner, suggested that Nixon should go on television to plead his case with the people of America. After all, the Republican National Committee had budgeted some TV time for the vice-presidential candidate.

Eisenhower's chief adviser, New York governor Tom Dewey, agreed to the plan in a phone call. Dewey said that at the end of the program Nixon should ask people to wire in their verdict. "If it is 60 percent for you and 40 percent against you, say you are getting out as that is not enough of a majority. If it is 90 to 10, stay on," Dewey said.

The thought of trying to get that kind of a massive "vote" of support from American television viewers depressed Nixon and his staff. It seemed impossible to do.

Then, Dwight Eisenhower finally called his running mate. Encouraging but cautious, Eisenhower said he had concluded that Nixon alone had to decide what to do next. "I don't want to be in the position of condemning an innocent man," he said. He urged Nixon to go on television to tell his story, to tell about his political life and how he had financed his career. Then Nixon asked if Eisenhower would be ready after the telecast to make an announcement one way or another, but Eisenhower would only say maybe.

Suddenly, all Nixon's anger and frustration over his ordeal bubbled out. "I told him that if he thought my staying on the ticket would be harmful, I would get off it and take the heat. But I also told him that there comes a time to stop dawdling, and that once I had done the television program he ought to decide," he later wrote, admitting that he also used an earthy, four-letter word in his conversation. After a long silence, Eisenhower said he had to wait a few days after the television show to decide. "Keep your chin up" were his parting words.[6]

Despite this neutral stand by Eisenhower, Nixon and his staff determined to put up a tough battle. The next day, Sunday, Nixon flew to Los Angeles, where the telecast was to take place on Tuesday, September 23. The Republican National Committee had paid $75,000 for a half hour of television time. Aboard the plane, Nixon sketched out ideas for his speech on blank postcards.

Meanwhile, news broke that the Democratic presidential candidate, Adlai Stevenson, had had his own special fund of $21,000, made up of money left over from his 1948 campaign for governor of Illinois plus contributions from businessmen and corporations. He had used some of the fund for campaign parties and gifts to newsmen. Some of the money had supplemented the salaries of staff members. But Nixon was furious that very few reporters asked Stevenson the same tough questions that he had to answer.

The next two days Nixon spent preparing his speech. He put together information about his own finances as well as a report done by an auditing firm on the fund. All the figures and facts had to be carefully memorized. A mistake on camera could be a disaster. "Why do you have to tell people how little we have and how much we owe?" Pat Nixon asked him. "People in political life have to live in a fish bowl," he replied.[7]

At 4:30 P.M. on Tuesday, Nixon was getting ready to leave for the television studio when he got another phone call from Tom Dewey. Dewey told him that Eisenhower's staff had just met and come to a decision. At the end of the broadcast, Nixon should announce that he was resigning from the ticket.

Nixon, who had been preparing to fight for his political life, was stunned. For several shocked seconds, he could not say a word. Did Eisenhower want him to resign as well? he asked. Dewey said that the advisers had not spoken directly to Eisenhower and that he had not yet approved their idea, but he was sure that Eisenhower had the same viewpoint.

"It's kind of late for them to pass on this kind of recommendation to me now," Nixon said. "I've already prepared my remarks, and it would be very difficult for me to change them now."[8]

Then Dewey suggested that Nixon resign from the Senate as well. The governor would have to call a special election for the empty Senate seat, Dewey said, and Nixon could run for it and vindicate himself by winning by a large margin.

Nixon erupted in fury. "Just tell them," he said, "that I haven't the slightest idea what I am going to do, and if they want to find out, they'd better listen to the broadcast. And tell them I know something about politics too!" He slammed down the phone.[9]

After making a few more notes on his speech, Nixon rode with Pat to the El Capitan Theater in Hollywood to arrive just twenty-five minutes before the broadcast. For the last few minutes before air time, Nixon and Pat sat in a dressing room waiting to go on. At one point he turned to her and said, "I just don't think I can go through with this one."

"Of course you can," she said, and took his hand, and they walked onstage together.[10]

A COCKER SPANIEL AND A CLOTH COAT

Onstage, she sat down in a print-covered armchair while he sat down at a French-provincial desk with his speech notes in front of him.

Once he began speaking, his face was a deadly serious, calm mask under brooding eyebrows. While 58 million Americans watched, almost everyone likely to vote in November, Nixon explained the fund and how he used it and how other senators and congressmen manipulated their expenses in order to get the government to pay for them. "Not one cent of the $18,000 or any other money of that type ever went to my personal use," he said.[11]

Two or three times, the camera focused on Pat, who sat still and smiling with her eyes fixed on her husband.

Nixon went on to detail exactly what he owned and owed. He had a 1950 Oldsmobile, $3,000 in equity in his house in California, and $20,000 in equity in a house in Washington. He still owed a total of $30,000 in mortgages on the two houses. "That's what we have. And that's what we owe. It isn't very much," he said. "But Pat and I have the satisfaction that every dime that we have got is honestly ours."

His wife didn't have a mink coat either, he said. "But she does have a respectable Republican cloth coat."[12]

Toward the end of his speech, Nixon told a story about one gift he did get after the nomination, a gift he planned to keep. A man in Texas sent them a little black-and-white cocker spaniel, and his girls had fallen in love with it. Six-year-old Tricia had named the dog Checkers. "I just want to say this, right now, that regardless of what they say about it, we are going to keep it," he said.[13]

It was very sentimental stuff, designed to tug at the hearts of the audience, and at home in front of their television sets, many of them found it very persuasive. Others found it syrupy sweet and corny. Many people who remembered nothing else about the speech recalled the remark about Pat Nixon's coat and the story about the dog. Forever after, this would be known as Nixon's "Checkers speech."

Finally, Nixon asked the audience to wire and write to the Republican National Committee with their opinions on whether he should resign or stay on the ticket, and said he would abide by their decision. By then, Nixon had talked so long he had run out of air time, and he failed to give the address for the National Committee. He was upset about ending the speech in a hurry, but his friends rushed up to congratulate him as he left the stage.

By the time they reached the hotel, total strangers were mobbing Nixon and his wife to shake their hands and pat them on the back. Meanwhile, viewers were wiring and writing to Republican offices all over the country. Some sent telegrams to Eisenhower and to his campaign offices. "The unofficial count was something between one and two million telegrams and letters containing more than three million names," Nixon said. "The response overwhelmingly was 'keep Nixon on the ticket.' "[14]

But while Nixon and his staff celebrated, still there was no direct word from Eisenhower about whether he wanted Nixon as his running mate anymore. Eisenhower had sent Nixon a telegram requesting that the two of them meet, but it got lost in the flood of telegrams from viewers. All Nixon saw was a news story in which Eisenhower said he had not yet made up his mind. "What more can he possibly want from me?" Nixon asked.[15]

Overwrought and impatient, Nixon had his secretary, Rose Mary Woods, type up a letter of resignation, but Murray Chotiner ripped it up. Finally, Nixon's staff persuaded him that he had to meet with Eisenhower at the general's next campaign stop in Wheeling, West Virginia. As soon as Nixon's plane landed, Eisenhower came striding down the aisle. "General," Nixon said, "you didn't need to come out to the airport." "Why not?" Eisenhower replied with a grin. "You're my boy."[16]

They went on to a rally at a nearby stadium where Eisenhower gave Nixon a stirring endorsement and announced that all members of the Republican National Committee who could be reached had voted to keep Nixon on the ticket.

Nixon had won another political victory, but he felt drained and tired. "It is said that you can live a year in a day.

That is how I felt about this period: I lived several years during that single week."

Pat Nixon was also deeply hurt. "I knew that from that time on, although she would do everything she could to help me and help my career, she would hate politics and dream of the day when I would leave it behind," Nixon said.[17]

Nor did the attacks end after that. In one newspaper column, false charges were made about a fraudulent tax return supposedly filed by the Nixons. Rumors were spread about Pat Nixon paying $10,000 cash to decorate the family home when in fact she had made many of the furnishings herself. On and on it went, right up until election day.

Nixon blamed most of the attacks on the enemies he had made during the Hiss case. But in fact, he had made many political enemies throughout his career, and he continued to do so during the 1952 campaign with sharp attacks on the Democrats. He was particularly reckless in his attempts to link the Democrats to Communism. Years later, he was sorry, particularly for the things he said about Dean Acheson, Truman's secretary of state.

In all, during the campaign Nixon and his wife traveled 46,000 miles (74,000 km) and visited 214 cities. They campaigned hard, long hours even when the polls said the Eisenhower-Nixon ticket had the election locked up.

On Election Day, Nixon voted early in the morning in East Whittier, then went out to the beach with a friend to play touch football. He went back to a Los Angeles hotel to take a nap that afternoon, but by 6:00 P.M. his excited friends and staff burst into the room to tell him the news. It had been a landslide. Eisenhower and Nixon had won by over a 6½-million-vote margin.

CHAPTER SEVEN

A VERY VISIBLE VICE PRESIDENT

A T 12:23 P.M. on January 23, 1953, Richard Nixon in striped morning trousers and a club coat stood with Pat before Senator William Knowland and laid his hand on two Bibles that had been in his mother's family for generations. As he took the oath of office for the vice presidency, his parents, Julie and Tricia, and other relatives sat in viewing stands nearby.

Nixon was barely forty years old, and it was just six years since he had arrived in Washington to serve in the House of Representatives. He and his wife still lived in a four-bedroom white-brick colonial house, just outside Washington, and in spite of Nixon's service in Congress, their lives were much like those of the typical suburban family. But soon things began to change. Five nights a week, they attended parties, dinners, and receptions. Tour buses drove down their street, and guides pointed out their home to tourists. A White House Cadillac and driver were at the Nixons' disposal, although it was mainly used by Nixon. Pat still drove to the supermarket to pick out her own vegetables and meat, but she did hire a five-day-a-week maid to help with the housework.

Nixon now mixed socially with kings and presidents and the wealthiest business executives. He even took up golf, a major pastime of Dwight Eisenhower, although Nixon never came to love the sport as the president did.

By this time Nixon had developed one particularly close friend, Charles "Bebe" Rebozo, the son of Cuban immigrants, who had made millions in the real estate business in Florida. After they met, in 1951, Nixon traveled often to Florida to spend time fishing on Rebozo's boat. Pat Nixon and her daughters also enjoyed Rebozo's company and often visited his home on Biscayne Bay. "Dick is comfortable with Bebe," Pat Nixon said. "He's almost like a brother to me, and Julie and Tricia look upon him as an uncle."[1]

Traditionally, the vice president stays in the background to the president, but Nixon thrust himself into the public eye like no vice president had before. Very soon after taking office, Eisenhower asked him to take a two-month trip through Asia, partly to strengthen ties to various countries but also to assess the deepening crisis in Indochina, then controlled by the French.

Nixon spent long hours preparing for the trip. Then on October 5, 1953, he and Pat departed, taking a staff of only seven people, far fewer than the huge crowds that now go on tour with U.S. officials. Among their stops were New Zealand and Australia, Indonesia, Korea, Japan, Cambodia, Laos, India and Pakistan, and the Philippines.

At one stop, in Burma, officials drove Nixon to a jungle temple to see a famous statue of Buddha. The local police warned that the visit might not be safe because of a Communist protest rally organized against Nixon, but Nixon insisted on walking to the shrine anyway. "No crowd of Communist demonstrators should be allowed to alter the itinerary of the Vice President of the United States," he decided. It was the same kind of stand he took many times throughout his life when faced with angry demonstrators.

He and Pat walked down the street with the Secret Service agents and Burmese police following them. As they headed into the sign-carrying crowd, Nixon approached one man and said, "I am Nixon, and I am glad to know you. What's your name?" The protester backed away in surprise, and Nixon approached other demonstrators. The protesters were embarrassed, and one by one the crowd began to melt away. Nixon had scored a political victory that made headlines in the United States.[2]

Frank and Hannah Nixon pose with their three children (left to right: Harold, Donald, and Richard) in this 1917 family portrait.

(Above) Nixon at Whittier College (center, standing). He was remembered as ''the most spirited bench warmer'' on the second-string football team. (Below) The Duke University School of Law, Class of 1937. Nixon is in back row at right.

Nixon (center) first achieved national prominence while still a congressman for his role in the House Un-American Activities Committee investigation of Alger Hiss, a former State Department official. Whittaker Chambers (left), a former Communist party member, testified that Hiss was also a Communist and had engaged in espionage activities. The man at the right is a committee investigator.

(Above) Nixon in 1950, with Pat at his side, gives an okay sign as he votes in the election that sent him to the U.S. Senate. (Above right) In 1952, General Dwight David Eisenhower (shown here with wife Mamie) chose Nixon to be his vice-presidential running mate. (Below right) Vice-presidential candidate Nixon, holding daughter Tricia, rides in a motorcade through his hometown of Whittier, California.

REPUBLICAN NATIONAL CONVENTION

SENATOR NIXON

The Owl Drug Co.
VISIT OUR FOUNTAIN
GOOD FOOD ~ RIGHT PRICES
YOUR Rexall DRUG STORE

MENS WEAR

Ken Mills
RETURN FOR MEN
DR. KENNETH F. PATTERSON
OPTOMETRIST

BAKERY

(Above) Nixon as vice president with his wife Pat and two daughters Tricia and Julie, vacationing on the New Jersey shore with their dog, Checkers. In his ''Checkers'' speech, made during the '52 campaign, Nixon defended himself against allegations that he made improper use of a fund set up for him by a group of businessmen. (Below) Demonstrators attack Vice President Nixon's car during his 1958 visit to Venezuela. The depth of anti-American feeling Nixon found in Latin America surprised him.

(Above) This well-known photo of the "kitchen debate" between Vice President Nixon and Soviet Premier Nikita Khrushchev held in the modern American kitchen of a model home was taken at a 1959 Moscow trade show. (Below) The jubilant Nixons at the 1960 Republican National Convention, where Nixon was nominated to be his party's presidential candidate.

(Above) The famous Kennedy-Nixon presidential debates of 1960 turned the tide in Kennedy's favor. Many believe they ushered in a new television-dominated era in American politics. (Below) Nixon concedes defeat to Kennedy in the 1960 presidential election, while Pat holds back tears.

In Vietnam, Nixon visited the jungle battlefields where the French and their Vietnamese allies faced the Communist-backed Vietminh guerrillas. The visit colored his opinions on Southeast Asia for decades to come. "I saw immediately a basic problem of the war," Nixon said. "The French did nothing to hide the disdain they felt toward the Vietnamese."[3]

He left Southeast Asia almost sure that the French would lose because they had not trained and inspired the Vietnamese to defend themselves. And if the French pulled out, Vietnam and possibly Laos and Cambodia would fall, he believed. "The United States would have to do everything possible to find a way to keep the French in Vietnam until the Communists had been defeated," he decided.[4]

Eventually, in April 1954, the French made their last stand in Vietnam at the garrison known as Dien Bien Phu. They wanted the United States to use its air power on the Communist forces, and the U.S. admiral who was chairman of the Joint Chiefs of Staff was ready to send B-29s on night raids around Dien Bien Phu. Nixon supported the plan, known as Operation Vulture, and tried to get Eisenhower's support. But Eisenhower refused to act unless Congress endorsed the plan. Nixon lobbied several key senators, but they rejected the idea.

After the fall of Dien Bien Phu, the French negotiated a settlement with the Vietminh. Eisenhower's secretary of state, John Foster Dulles, refused to let the United States sign the agreement because it called for surrendering half of Vietnam to the Communists. "Dulles and I both believed," Nixon said, "that if the Communists pushed too far we would have to do whatever was necessary to stop them."[5]

One key role for Nixon during his early days in the vice presidency was serving as a go-between for Eisenhower with Joseph McCarthy, the maverick Republican senator from Wisconsin, who like Nixon had built a reputation as a fighter of Communists. But McCarthy took wild swings at various government employees with little proof to back up his charges. On the one hand, Nixon tried to talk McCarthy out of attacking various officials, but he also tried to convince

Eisenhower that the White House had to consider each of McCarthy's charges on its merits instead of tossing them all out wholesale.

In April 1954, however, McCarthy made a fatal mistake by launching an investigation of Communism in the Army. The ex–Army general, Eisenhower, was appalled by McCarthy's attempt to subpoena top military officials to appear before his committee. Nixon failed to persuade McCarthy to tone down his harsh approach. Eventually, Eisenhower had Nixon make a speech that disavowed McCarthy, although McCarthy was never mentioned by name.

Public opinion began to swing against McCarthy. As people watched the Army-McCarthy hearings on television, they realized how little truth his charges had. In December, the Senate censured McCarthy for his behavior during the hearings and for other indiscretions. He had made the fatal mistake of criticizing other members of Congress.

Nixon also lost faith in McCarthy after the senator's attacks on the Eisenhower administration. "It is despicable to make a racket of anticommunism or any other cause," Nixon said, "to stir people up and then give them no positive leadership or direction."[6]

One Saturday afternoon in September 1955, Nixon had sat down in his living room to read the sports pages when the phone rang. On the line was Eisenhower's press secretary. "Dick," said the voice, "this is Jim Hagerty—the President has had a coronary."[7] Eisenhower had had a heart attack while on a trip to Denver and had gone into an Army hospital.

Nixon sat in stunned silence at first. Then he called an Eisenhower Cabinet member, Bill Rogers, and asked him to come to his house. Once Rogers had arrived, reporters began ringing the Nixon doorbell. Soon television cameras were stationed on the sidewalk and floodlights shone on the house.

Pat went to the door to tell the reporters her husband wasn't home. Nixon felt he wasn't ready to answer questions about Eisenhower's condition because he knew very little about it, and he also didn't want anyone to think he was barging in and trying to assume power. Still, he didn't want to look like a political weakling unable to handle the crisis.

What he wanted first was a couple of hours of privacy to plan his next moves. He and Rogers ducked out the back door and ran through a neighbor's yard to where Rogers's car was parked. Then Rogers drove Nixon to his home to spend the night.

There Nixon used a kitchen wall phone to call Denver to learn more about the president's condition. Nixon helped arrange for civilian doctors to examine Eisenhower in addition to the Army doctors already involved. He also discussed with Eisenhower's advisers how the day-to-day government should run during the president's absence. The U.S. Constitution had no specific instructions for such situations. Nixon and the others decided that they would take a "team" approach based in part on a staff system Eisenhower had set up.

For the next two weeks, Nixon was careful to do all his business in his own office rather than in Eisenhower's. When he had to see Cabinet members, he went to their offices rather than summoning them to his. He presided over meetings of the National Security Council and Cabinet, but declined to sit in Eisenhower's chair. Still he didn't satisfy everyone. Some Cabinet members said he was doing too much, and some told him he wasn't doing enough.

But the experience raised his standing in the eyes of the press and other politicians. "A bandwagon of sorts had started the very first week," Nixon said, "but I knew how fickle that sort of support could be."[8]

In spite of how well he had done, doubts clouded plans for his future. Although Eisenhower recovered from his heart attack, many questioned whether Eisenhower could run for re-election in 1956 in light of his illness. If he didn't, what would happen to Nixon? Would he try for the presidency himself?

Then Eisenhower began wavering about whether Nixon should be his running mate again. Eisenhower had always regarded their relationship as that of a father dealing with an immature son. Several of the president's advisers did not like

Nixon and told Eisenhower that the political polls showed that Nixon would cost Eisenhower some votes in 1956.

On December 26, 1955, Eisenhower called Nixon into the Oval Office and suggested to him that instead of running for vice president again, Nixon should step down and take a Cabinet post, possibly that of secretary of defense.

Nixon was stunned and felt that Eisenhower's advisers had "set him up." Several more times, Eisenhower made the same suggestion, and each time Nixon gave the same answer: "If you believe your own candidacy and your administration would be better served with me off the ticket, you tell me what you want me to do and I'll do it. I want to do what is best for you."

But Eisenhower never seemed ready to take a firm stand. He always answered: "No, I think we've got to do what's best for you."[9]

When Eisenhower finally announced officially, on February 29, 1956, that he would run again, reporters bombarded him with the question, Would Richard Nixon run for vice president again, too? Eisenhower did not say yes or no and told reporters to wait for the convention.

Soon the news magazines and papers began speculating that Eisenhower was planning to dump Nixon. The next few weeks were torture for Nixon. Finally, after another presidential press conference in which Eisenhower told the press that he had told Nixon "to chart his own course," Nixon thought about quitting the ticket to join a New York law firm. "It's a question of either/or," he told some of Eisenhower's advisers. "Remain vice president or get out of politics."[10]

Meanwhile, the presidential primaries had begun. In New Hampshire, a Republican senator who supported Nixon called his friends urging them to write Nixon's name on the primary ballot as presidential nominee. In the end, Eisenhower got 56,464 votes and Nixon got almost 23,000. Suddenly, Nixon didn't look like such a drag on the ticket anymore.

In April Eisenhower finally told the press that he was simply waiting for Nixon to decide whether to run. The next day Nixon made an appointment to see Eisenhower to give him the word. "Mr. President," he said, "I would be honored to continue as Vice President under you."[11]

Nixon was renominated at the convention by a vote of 1,323 to 1. Shortly afterward, his father died after a long and painful illness. His doctor told Nixon that only the determination to see his son win the fight for renomination had kept his father alive at the end.

As the campaign began in 1956 against Adlai Stevenson, again the Democratic nominee, Eisenhower urged Nixon to be less aggressive in attacking the Democrats, to concentrate instead on pointing out the accomplishments of the Republicans. It was a new and more conciliatory Richard Nixon on the campaign trail, and the press was surprised. This time it was Stevenson and the Democrats who called Nixon names: "the White House pet midget" and "the vice-hatchet man."[12] But for the most part, Nixon refused to respond in kind.

Of course, the polls did show the Eisenhower-Nixon ticket with a solid lead throughout the campaign. On election eve, in one last desperate shot, Stevenson made a speech that implied that Eisenhower might not live through the next four years and the country might soon have Nixon as president. The next day, Eisenhower and Nixon chalked up another landslide vote, taking forty-one of the then forty-eight states.

But Eisenhower's health was still fragile. In November 1957, he suffered a stroke, which at first seemed very serious. He managed to recover almost fully except for a mild speech impairment that sometimes made it hard for him to find the right words to express himself.

A few months later, Eisenhower sent Nixon on a trip to South America. The continent did not interest Nixon very much but the trip would have a major effect on his career. Plans were for him to visit every country in South America except for Brazil and Chile in two and a half weeks and to be in Argentina for the inauguration of a new president, Arturo Frondizi.

The first stops were in Uruguay, Argentina, Paraguay, and Bolivia, where there were some polite anti-American demonstrations. But for the most part, warm, welcoming crowds cheered the Nixons.

In Peru, the situation was murkier. The government of Peru was shaky and so was its economy. Many Peruvians were angry with the United States for supposedly "dumping" surplus cotton on the world market and driving down the price of Peru's chief export.

Once Nixon reached his hotel in Lima, his staff warned him that Communists were passing out thousands of leaflets urging students and workers to gather for an anti-Nixon protest at San Marcos University, where Nixon was supposed to speak. Should he cancel the visit? Nixon asked Peruvian officials. They told him they feared violence, but would not tell him to stay away from the university.

Nixon spent an almost sleepless night trying to decide whether to go or not. "If I did go, I would have a chance to demonstrate that the United States does not shrink from its responsibilities or flee in the face of threats," he later wrote.[13]

Leaving Pat at the hotel the next morning, Nixon went to a wreath-laying ceremony at the tomb of General José de San Martín, the "George Washington" of Peru. He got back in his car and ordered the driver to go to the university. Two blocks from the university plaza, the group in the motorcade began to hear the mob yelling, *Fuera Nixon!* ("Go Home, Nixon!") and *Muera Nixon!* ("Death to Nixon!").

Fifty yards (46 m) from the university's front gate, Nixon and two staff members left the car and walked toward the crowd of 2,000 demonstrators. At first the protesters seemed to quiet down, then suddenly the three Americans felt rocks whizzing by them. Nixon's Secret Service aide was hit in the mouth with a rock that broke a front tooth. Nixon and the two men returned quickly to their car, but as they drove away, Nixon stood up in the convertible and shouted, "You are cowards, you are afraid of the truth!"[14]

They went on to another, more sympathetic university where Nixon spoke to a more receptive crowd.

Back at their hotel, an angry crowd also tried to block the Nixon party's way to the door. One demonstrator even spit in Nixon's face. Nixon's Secret Service man grabbed the protester. "As I saw his legs go by," Nixon said, "I at least had the satisfaction of planting a healthy kick on his shins. Nothing I did all day made me feel better."[15]

In Venezuela, the situation grew even more ugly. The Venezuelans were angry at the United States for giving asylum to a dictator who had been recently ousted, and the Communists were organizing massive demonstrations against Nixon's visit.

At the airport in Caracas, Nixon and his wife disembarked, to be met by government officials on the runway. On the observation deck of the airport terminal, an angry mob waved banners and screamed insults. As the Nixons approached the terminal, hundreds of people spit tobacco juice at them. Ugly, dark blotches soon covered their clothes.

Along with various Venezuelan officials, they rushed to the limousines outside. Nixon was in one car; Pat was in another, riding behind him. They drove slowly through the crowd with the windows tightly rolled up despite the stifling heat. Then suddenly they hit a roadblock, several vehicles deliberately parked in the center of the street. Hundreds of screaming people swooped down to attack the motorcade with rocks and sticks.

Secret Service agents on the sides of the cars tried to push away the demonstrators as they yelled, *"Muera Nixon!"* The Venezuelan foreign minister, who was in the car with Nixon, kept saying, "This is terrible, this is terrible."

When the mob started to bash the windows with iron pipes and rock the limousine, the Secret Service man in the car with Nixon pulled his revolver but Nixon grabbed his arm. "I knew intuitively that the firing of a gun would be the excuse for the mob to get completely out of hand," he later said.[16]

Somehow, the drivers turned the cars around to drive to the U.S. embassy, where the Nixons took refuge, instead of to a government guesthouse where they were supposed to stay.

Still the mobs roamed the streets, and the news that managed to get back to Washington frightened Eisenhower. He sent troops to several Caribbean bases near Venezuela so that they could be available if needed. Nixon was upset by this troop movement and announced that the Venezuelan government could certainly handle the situation without outside help.

Many Caracas citizens sent their apologies to the Nixons, and the government officials insisted on giving them a special luncheon. But the Nixons left as soon as they politely could.

When the Nixons arrived back home in Washington, 15,000 people were at the National Airport to greet them, including President Eisenhower, the Cabinet, and Democratic and Republican leaders of Congress. The trip that Nixon had thought would be dull had given his career a tremendous lift.

Nixon's courage in the face of angry mobs boosted his popularity in the press and among the public. One month after he got back, the polls showed him running in a virtual tie with John F. Kennedy, expected to run against Nixon for president in 1960.

Another foreign trip that also won favorable publicity for Nixon was his visit to Moscow to meet with Premier Nikita Khrushchev in 1959. Khrushchev was something of a reformer in Russia compared with the previous dictator, Joseph Stalin, and had greatly increased cultural and political contact with the West, but he was still a tough and belligerent leader.

Officially, Nixon went to Moscow to open the first United States Exhibition ever held in the Soviet Union. As part of his visit, Nixon toured the exhibit at Sokolniki Park with Khrushchev. As they walked around the grounds, more than a hundred members of the press tagged along, and here and there, Khrushchev, very aware of the reporters, stopped to throw an insult at Nixon or the United States. Nixon, trying to be polite, attempted to change the subject and to talk about the color television and other products on display in the exhibit.

"He had gone after me with no holds barred," Nixon said later. "And I had had to counter him like a fighter with one hand tied behind his back."

Walking by a model American grocery store, Nixon said his father once owned a store and that he and his brothers had worked there. Khrushchev snapped: "Oh, all shopkeepers are thieves."[17]

Finally, they entered the model kitchen of the American home set up in the middle of the exhibit. Soviet reporters had complained that no American worker could ever afford such a palace. There Nixon took on Khrushchev in what was later called their "kitchen conference." For the first time, Nixon began to get the best of Khrushchev in their argument.

Nixon pointed out that a steelworker in the United States could easily buy such a house, which cost only $14,000. Khrushchev insisted that steelworkers and peasants could have similar housing in the Soviet Union.

Nixon started talking about freedom of choice in the United States and about the many builders there producing homes and factories turning out washing machines. Khrushchev said it was better to have one model of washing machine than many.

"Yes that's the kind of competition we want," Khrushchev said, "but your generals say we must compete in rockets."

"To me, you are strong and we are strong," Nixon replied. "If war comes we both lose."[18]

The discussion went on and on until they began to talk about the need to relieve Cold War tensions. Both men agreed that they wanted peace and that they wanted a peace conference that was going on in Geneva to be a success.

Pictures of the two in their head-to-head debate on Communism and democracy ran on front pages of papers worldwide.

CHAPTER EIGHT

A CHANCE AT
THE WHITE HOUSE

W H I L E Eisenhower was in the White House, Nixon traveled thousands of miles to campaign for would-be senators, congressmen, and state legislators. This steadily built up political debts to Nixon that he knew someday would be repaid if he ran for president.

He wasn't known for his charm and humor, but he was making friends. William Bagley, running for the state Senate in California in 1960, talked his way into a reception for Nixon at a San Francisco hotel. "I really wanted to get my picture taken with the vice president so I could use it during my campaign," Bagley said.

Bagley stood forlornly at the end of a line of people grouped around Nixon for a picture when Nixon told him, "Bill, put your arm on the guy next to you and extend it over his shoulder. That way they won't cut you out of the photo."

"Of course, it was all calculated to pay off when Nixon ran for president," Bagley said.[1]

The only other candidate in 1960 with a shot at the Republican nomination for president was Nelson Rockefeller, the governor of New York, a far more liberal politician than Nixon. But Rockefeller didn't run in the primaries, and he eventually declined to run for the nomination.

Meanwhile, on the Democratic side, a strong candidate was emerging, John F. Kennedy, who had been elected to Congress in the same year as Nixon. As Kennedy moved from primary to primary beating out the other front-runner, Senator Hubert Humphrey, in tough races, he drew much more public attention than Nixon, who breezed along in the ho-hum Republican primaries.

During the first week of July 1960, the Democrats met in Los Angeles and chose Kennedy as their candidate on the first ballot. He in turn picked Lyndon Baines Johnson, the Senate majority leader from Texas, as his running mate. The choice was designed to win the votes of Northern liberals and Southern conservatives. "I insisted from the outset that Kennedy was most likely to be nominated and would be the hardest to beat," Nixon said.[2]

By the time the Republicans met in Chicago, in late July, the Kennedy-Johnson ticket had pulled slightly ahead in the polls. On Wednesday, July 27, Nixon was unanimously chosen as his party's nominee. Rockefeller declined Nixon's invitation to be the vice-presidential candidate, and Nixon chose Henry Cabot Lodge of Massachusetts, the U.S. ambassador to the United Nations.

The next evening Nixon gave an acceptance speech promising to follow through on what Eisenhower had done and to take new action as well. He pledged to fight racial prejudice but also to fight Communism. He also promised to visit all fifty states during his campaign. In closing, he used a quote from Lincoln, whom he admired greatly:

> *A hundred years ago, Abraham Lincoln was asked during the dark days of the tragic War Between the States whether he thought God was on his side. His answer was "My concern is not whether God is on our side, but whether we are on God's side."*
>
> *My fellow Americans, may that ever be our prayer for our country. And in that spirit, with faith in America, with faith in her ideals and in her people, I accept your nomination for President of the United States.*[3]

Although Kennedy was of Nixon's generation and came to Congress in the same year, the contrast between the two men was sharp. Kennedy was a product of East Coast wealth and liberalism, his father was a millionaire, and the young Kennedy had gone to Harvard. Nixon, although he had gone to an Eastern law school, was identified with the West, and he delighted in telling audiences that his father had owned a grocery store and that he had had to work his way through college.

The press quickly focused on Kennedy's youth, charm, and quick wit and his apparent devotion to his graceful, beautiful young wife. Reporters neglected to mention or overlooked his affairs with other women. The Nixons, on the other hand, often came across to the press as too intense and hardworking, lacking in a sense of fun and humor. As Pat Nixon told one reporter, "We both work hard; we are both self-sufficient; we don't show temper or irritation. We are friendly and try to give off warmth."[4]

Although Kennedy suffered from severe back pain and had a chronic illness that required treatment with cortisone, he looked as if he were the more athletic and energetic of the two candidates. That impression seemed to be confirmed when Nixon bumped his knee while getting into a car during a campaign trip to North Carolina. By August 27, ten days later, his leg was so swollen and painful he had to enter Walter Reed Army Hospital for tests. The doctors ordered massive doses of antibiotics for the candidate plus two weeks in bed.

Nixon was devastated. Just as the campaign was heating up, he was tied to a hospital bed while Kennedy was crossing the country, winning votes.

Nixon's campaign advisers urged him to drop his campaign pledge that he would visit every state, but he stubbornly refused to do so. While he was in the hospital, Kennedy had taken a slim lead in the polls, so Nixon decided that he had to increase his campaign load to try to regain lost ground.

Nixon kept rolling up the miles: fourteen states in his first week out of the hospital; eleven states in the second. The pace took its toll. He lost 10 pounds (4.5 kg) and still had a fever intermittently. His clothes hung on him; his face looked pale and tired.

One personal difference between the candidates quickly turned into a major issue although both Kennedy and Nixon refused to discuss it. Kennedy was a Catholic, and no Catholic had ever been elected president before. Although some Protestants wondered whether the pope could have an influence on Kennedy's decision-making if he sat in the Oval Office, Nixon defended Kennedy's loyalty to his country. "I, personally, would never raise the question and would not tolerate any use of the religious issue by anyone connected with my campaign," Nixon said.[5]

Nixon personally believed that the religious issue might actually help Kennedy in the election, particularly in the more urban, heavily populated states where Kennedy needed to win big.

Eventually, Kennedy made a key speech to a group of ministers in Houston which managed to convince many voters that he believed firmly in the separation of church and state and that his religion need have no influence over his actions as president.

Early in the campaign, a proposal was made that the two candidates appear jointly for debates on nationwide radio and television. Kennedy was eager for the debates, but Nixon's advisers were not so sure. Nixon was better known, and television would simply provide Kennedy with a wider audience. Not only that, but Nixon was also an incumbent vice president, which meant that Kennedy could go on the attack and Nixon would have to defend the record of the current president.

But Nixon believed that he could not say no without his refusal becoming a major campaign issue. As a champion debater in college and high school, he also must have felt that he had the edge in a one-on-one meeting with his opponent.

The first debate was set for Monday, September 26, in Chicago, just a little over two weeks after Nixon left the hospital. Still worn out physically, Nixon arrived in Chicago late the night before the debate and then had to travel to several rallies on his way from the airport to his hotel. He didn't get to bed until well after one o'clock Monday morning.

The next morning Kennedy relaxed in his hotel room and talked to his advisers, who briefed him on the kinds of questions he might have to answer in the debate. Meanwhile, Nixon was out making a campaign appearance at a union hall, even though it was a group that was sure to endorse Kennedy. In the afternoon, Nixon finally sat down for five hours to review material put together by his staff.

While Kennedy and his advisers seemed to be looking forward to the debate, tension rose in the Nixon camp. As he rode to the television station, Nixon studied his notes and spoke little to his staff. Still Nixon felt thoroughly prepared to do battle with the facts and figures he had crammed into his head.

Looking pale and tired, Nixon arrived at the studio first. Because of the weight he had lost, his shirt collar hung loosely around his neck. An adviser suggested that he wear heavy television makeup, but he refused. Instead, he allowed only a light pancake makeup to be dusted over his persistent five o'clock shadow of beard.

Kennedy on the other hand was tanned and well-rested. When TV producers suggested that his white shirt might create a glare on camera, he sent back to the hotel to get a blue shirt to put on instead.

Then the men took their seats, the cameras focused on them, and history was made. The moderator, Howard K. Smith, announced, "The television and radio stations of the United States ... are proud to provide for a discussion of issues in the current political campaign by the two major candidates for the presidency."[6]

As the two men gave their opening statements, Kennedy seemed smoother, calmer, more aggressive on camera. Nixon seemed to be on the defensive, trying to refute and rebut Kennedy, rather than giving Americans his vision of a better world.

Nixon still looked weak and haggard from his illness. He perspired heavily on camera, and sweat streaked the light powder on his cheeks. After the debate, his mother even phoned his campaign advisers to ask if he was ill.

Riding back in the car to his hotel, even Nixon had the feeling that he had lost the debate, based on appearances at least. "I should have remembered that 'A picture is worth a thousand words,'" he said.[7]

Postdebate polls gave the edge to Kennedy although those who had heard the debate on the radio said Nixon had won. This was small comfort to Nixon, since five or six times as many people had watched the debate on television.

In an effort to improve his appearance for the next television outing, Nixon began drinking milkshakes to regain some of the weight he had lost. In subsequent debates he used theatrical makeup. The next debate also dealt with foreign affairs—Nixon's strongest area—instead of domestic policy, which was the subject of the first debate.

As a result, after the second debate on October 7, commentators and polls called Nixon the winner. Nixon also did well in the third and fourth debates, but the audience for the second through fourth debates was never as large as that for the first. And somehow the first debate put more sparkle into the Kennedy campaign even though the polls said the debates had little effect on the election. Beginning the morning after that first TV meeting with Nixon, Kennedy's on-the-street crowds began to grow in size and excitement.

Just before the fourth debate, Kennedy came out with a surprising stand that seemed aimed at making him look like more of an anti-Communist than Nixon. He called for the United States government to aid Cuban exiles and rebels who hoped to overthrow the pro-Communist regime of Cuban dictator Fidel Castro.

As vice president, Nixon knew that the U.S. Central Intelligence Agency was already aiding the rebels. He also found out that Kennedy had been briefed by the Central Intelligence Agency about this aid. Nixon favored the aid, but felt that if he said so and admitted that the government was already training the exiles for an invasion of Cuba, he would endanger the secrecy of the operation.

So during the debate, he argued the opposite that such aid would be wrong and irresponsible would violate treaty agreements and lose friends America. His attack was so successful that he ended ting favorable stories written about him by editorial and columnists who generally favored Kennedy. thought Kennedy had been off-base with his new 'tough' line on Cuba," he said.[8]

After the debates, Nixon stepped up his campaigning to fulfill his pledge to cover all fifty states. In late October, many newspapers and magazines began to predict that Kennedy would win by a wide margin.

As he crisscrossed the country, Nixon seemed unable to build momentum in his campaign. His speeches were tainted with self-pity. He seemed to identify with the losers of the world as he talked about how his mother rose early in the morning to bake pies so that he and his brothers could get an education or how he never made the football first-string at Whittier. To those who watched the Nixons on the road in these last few weeks, husband and wife looked terribly tired.

In the waning days of the campaign, another incident aided Kennedy. On October 26, the civil rights leader Dr. Martin Luther King, Jr. was sentenced to four months of hard labor in state prison following his arrest in a restaurant sit-in in Atlanta. Although Southern Democrats warned Kennedy not to get involved, he called Mrs. King to express his concern and promised to help. His brother Robert Kennedy phoned the Georgia judge who had given the sentence and persuaded him to set bail so that King could be released pending appeal.

Nixon also took action but felt it would be improper for him to call the judge. Instead he asked the U.S. attorney general to try to get White House approval so that the Justice Department could intervene in the case. But the Eisenhower administration refused to back such a move.

So black leaders across the country endorsed Kennedy. The civil rights leader's father, Martin Luther King, Sr., a Baptist minister who had previously endorsed Nixon, now switched his vote to Kennedy. "I've got a suitcase of votes," the older King said, "and I'm going to take them to Mr. Kennedy and dump them in his lap."[9]

The sad part for Nixon was that he had fought for civil rights legislation in the Eisenhower administration and had worked to develop a program involving government contracts to provide many jobs for blacks. These efforts were ignored.

Throughout most of the campaign, Eisenhower had stayed largely in the background, doing little campaigning. Many people thought this was due to Nixon's fierce determination to be on his own with no interference from the president. Others felt Eisenhower was not that enthusiastic about Nixon. But actually, Nixon contended that he always intended to use Eisenhower heavily during the last two weeks of the campaign.

Just before the election, Eisenhower proposed making many appearances for Nixon, but Mamie Eisenhower was seriously worried about what this would do to her husband's health. Mrs. Eisenhower called Pat Nixon and urged that Nixon try to talk the president out of the heavy campaign schedule. "Ike must never know I called you," she said.

The next day at lunch, Nixon made a number of what he called "lame excuses" for why Eisenhower should not make all the campaign appearances he had planned. "His pride prevented him from saying anything, but I knew that he was puzzled and frustrated by my conduct," Nixon said.[10]

In the few appearances he ended up making for Nixon in the final week, Eisenhower attracted huge crowds and made a powerful impression. Many felt that if he had campaigned more for Nixon, it would have changed the outcome of the race.

Despite all the obstacles, Nixon felt he had gained strength in his last week on the road. He was upbeat and believed he might pull out a victory after all.

During the last weekend before the election, Nixon started a final blitz. Beginning on Sunday, he went seventy-two hours with only five hours of sleep. From California, he flew to Alaska, and then to Madison, Wisconsin, and then to Detroit. On Monday, he held a four-hour afternoon nationwide telethon. During that time, he answered questions from callers all over the country. "I was tired physically," he said, "but despite lack of sleep, I had never felt more alert mentally and none of the questions gave me any trouble."[11]

After a final election eve broadcast in Chicago, he flew to Los Angeles to vote and await the returns. During the campaign he had traveled 65,000 miles (104,600 km) and given 180 scheduled speeches.

The next morning, after voting in Whittier, Nixon left his wife and daughters behind and he and some campaign advisers drove down the Pacific Coast Highway to Tijuana for lunch and sightseeing. Throughout the day, Nixon did not turn on the car radio because he didn't want to hear the first returns from the East, where he knew Kennedy would be strong. But by the time he returned to his hotel in Los Angeles, he was getting anxious and called a staff member for an analysis of the first returns. He was in a suite on the fourth floor; his wife and daughters were in a fifth-floor suite.

During the night, several states swung back and forth, and it was clear that there would not be a Kennedy landslide. But by six, before the polls even closed on the West Coast, CBS predicted that Kennedy had won. But the Nixon forces held on to a slim hope as such states as Kentucky, Vermont, Oklahoma, Arizona, and Florida went for Nixon.

Seven large states were keys to the election—New York, Pennsylvania, Ohio, Michigan, Illinois, Texas, and California. Of those, Nixon calculated he had to carry at least three to win. Later in the evening, Kennedy was winning in New York, Pennsylvania, Michigan, and Texas while Nixon won Ohio. So Nixon's hopes rested heavily on California, where votes would be the last to be counted, and Illinois, where Democratic mayor Richard Daley was holding off announcement of the Chicago returns until the downstate heavily Republican voting was totaled up.

Meanwhile, although Kennedy was ahead in the electoral vote, his popular vote lead was shrinking, and Nixon swept up state after state in the farm belt and Middle West. By ten-thirty, Kennedy's popular-vote lead was only 1.1 million votes.

Still all the commentators and many newspapers were talking about what Nixon would do after he lost the election, and many newsmen wondered why Nixon had not conceded. At eleven-thirty, Nixon decided he had to make some kind of statement, even if he didn't admit defeat. Pat and Tricia walked into Nixon's suite, and fourteen-year-old Tricia asked, "Hi, Daddy, how's the election coming?"

When he answered, "I'm afraid we've lost," Tricia burst into tears. "I'm not crying because of myself," she said, "but for you and Mommy. You have worked so long and hard."[12]

When he told Pat that he was going down to the hotel ballroom to thank his workers and tell them that if the voting trends continued, Kennedy would probably win, she refused to go along at first. But a few minutes later, she told her husband, who was drafting his speech, "I think we should go down together."[13]

Shortly after midnight, the Nixons walked onto the ballroom stage while the crowd called out, "Don't give up!" Nixon's face was stony, and Pat's eyes shone with tears. Nixon barely got out his statement: "If the present trend continues, Senator Kennedy will be the next President."[14] As quickly as they could, the Nixons left.

But the painful agony of what might have been and almost was continued as Nixon combed final reports and his advisers held out hope for victory. At four he went to bed and then awoke at six to find out voting fraud had been reported in Chicago and Texas and many Republicans were demanding recounts. Kennedy's margin of victory was razor thin. He received 34,221,000 votes to Nixon's 34,108,000. A change of a half vote per precinct could have changed the outcome. Kennedy received 303 electoral votes to Nixon's 219.

Some advised Nixon to demand a recount before records could be destroyed. But Nixon knew that such a count could take months and might throw a shadow over Kennedy's administration. He didn't want to subject the country to such an ordeal nor did he want to be labeled as a sore loser. There was nothing left but to admit to Kennedy: "I know that you will have the united support of all Americans as you lead the nation in the cause of peace and freedom during the next four years."[15] Even lifelong critics of Nixon admired his decision not to put the country through a constitutional crisis over the vote.

Reviewing the campaign later, Nixon felt that he had worked too hard and traveled too many miles. He should have saved himself for the major events. He also believed, "I paid too much attention to what I was going to say and too little to how I would look."[16]

One bad camera angle on television had more effect on a campaign, he decided, than a major mistake in a speech. In future elections, he predicted television would play an even bigger role in winning votes.

He also came away with an increased uneasiness about the press and what reporters thought of him. He believed that most reporters were liberals at heart and would deliberately slant their stories if they liked a candidate. "Kennedy's organization approached campaign dirty tricks with a roguish relish and carried them off with an insouciance that captivated many politicians and overcame the critical faculties of many reporters," he said.[17]

Of course, there was a bit of truth behind all this; reporters covering Kennedy had been wildly enthusiastic about the Democratic candidate. But Nixon's anger and bitterness only tended to increase the barriers between him and the press.

As Nixon's last few months as vice president drew to a close, he had to decide what to do next: he had to find a job. Except for their Washington home, the Nixons had little to fall back on financially. But job offers poured in, and he decided to join the law firm of Adams, Duque & Hazeltine of Los Angeles.

Then came the final hours in office on January 30, 1961. After the inaugural ceremony for Kennedy and a farewell luncheon for Eisenhower, the Nixons had a quiet dinner at home.

Nixon still had use of his official car and chauffeur until midnight, and after dinner, he asked the driver to take him for one last ride to the Capitol.

Once there, he walked to the rotunda, covered by the Capitol dome, and then out onto the balcony above the Capitol mall. Looking out across the snow-covered mall, he could see the Washington Monument and Lincoln Memorial standing stark and beautiful against a gray sky. Events of his years in Washington passed quickly through his mind. "As I turned to go inside," Nixon said, "I suddenly stopped short, struck by the thought that this was not the end—that someday I would be back here."[18]

CHAPTER NINE

BACK TO CALIFORNIA

T H E next few months were a period of difficult adjustment for Richard Nixon. Eventually he would realize that he would never learn to like life outside politics, that he would never adjust to simply being a lawyer again.

He moved to Los Angeles and rented a small apartment near his new office, while Pat remained in Washington waiting for the girls to finish the school year. For several weeks, he had trouble concentrating on his new job with the law firm. "Everything I did seemed unexciting and unimportant by comparison with national office," he said.[1]

Still the financial rewards were greater than in Washington. His annual salary totaled $100,000, and he soon began writing a syndicated newspaper column for another $40,000 a year. He also signed a contract to write his first book. He made more money that first year than in all his years in Washington as a public official.

The book, *Six Crises,* became a best-seller and dealt with the major turning points in his life: the Alger Hiss Case, the funds crisis and Checkers speech, his visit to Venezuela, Eisenhower's illnesses, his meeting with Khrushchev, and the 1960 presidential campaign.

After the Nixons failed to find a house to buy, they decided to build one themselves in the luxurious Bel Air section of Los Angeles. The ranch-style home cost $100,000 and had four bedrooms, seven baths, and a swimming pool.

While they waited for it to be completed, the Nixons rented the home of a movie producer in Brentwood.

Although he was out of office, Nixon thought of himself as the head of the opposition party, the man who should lead criticism of what the Democratic administration was doing.

Then in mid-April, the new president, John F. Kennedy, was embroiled in crisis. Rebel forces, trained and financed by the United States, had landed at the Bay of Pigs in Cuba. They aimed to lead a revolution and wrest power away from dictator Fidel Castro. But the invaders were quickly crushed.

Nixon heard from government sources that Kennedy had ordered the invasion against his staff's advice. But as a compromise with those who opposed the invasion, Kennedy had canceled some of the U.S. air strikes intended to protect the rebels and hold off the Cuban air force. Nixon and Republicans in Congress decided that they had to stand behind Kennedy during the crisis, and Kennedy soon called Nixon to the White House for his advice.

"What would you do now in Cuba?" Kennedy asked.

"I would find a proper legal cover and I would go in," Nixon replied. ". . . I believe that the most important thing at this point is that we do whatever is necessary to get Castro and communism out of Cuba."[2] Nixon promised to support Kennedy completely if he invaded Cuba. But Kennedy did not take Nixon's advice.

Meanwhile, friends and party members around the country were urging Nixon to run for governor of California in 1962 against the incumbent Democrat, Edmund G. "Pat" Brown, Sr. (Brown was also the father of a future governor and presidential candidate, Jerry Brown.) After all, the polls showed that Nixon had a twenty-point lead over Brown, and Nixon had carried California in the presidential election.

Nixon's intuition told him he should not run, but he also knew he wanted to get back into politics. He sought advice of trusted friends and some of them, like Robert Finch and H. R. "Bob" Haldeman, told him not to get into the race.

Brown was not an enormously popular politician, but he had taken some steps that people liked. He had expanded the state's university system and had found new sources of water for southern California.

Nixon also was not sure that he was interested in statewide issues of water and planning and highways. His focus had always been the national and international scene, and governors had very little to do with that. "The real problem," he said, "was that I had no great desire to be governor of California."[3]

But if he didn't run, some Republicans told him, he might be out of politics forever. Eisenhower told Nixon: "If you don't run and the Republican candidate loses, you will be blamed for it, and you will be through as a national political leader."[4]

While Nixon weighed the pros and cons of the race with others, he did not discuss the matter with his family. Pat was fiercely opposed, he knew, to his return to politics. She wanted a private life with no more intrusions by the press, and she wanted him to provide a more normal home life for Tricia and Julie. Knowing how strongly Pat opposed his re-entering politics, he put off talking about it with her and the girls until two days before a press conference on his decision.

Some friends claimed that when he told her, the couple had a violent quarrel. But according to Julie Nixon Eisenhower, the family discussed the matter at the table one evening after dinner and then voted on whether he should run. Pat and Tricia said no while Julie voted yes, and Pat said she wouldn't campaign for him if he went ahead with the race. Nixon seemed to accept the decision. "That is life," he told them. "You don't always win." Then he left for his room. That's when Tricia told her mother, "If it means so much to Daddy, maybe we should change our votes."[5]

First Tricia and then Pat told Nixon they had changed their minds. Pat sat down on a sofa near his desk and said, "I am more convinced than ever that if you run, it will be a terrible mistake. But if you weigh everything and still decide to run, I will support your decision. I'll be there campaigning with you just as I always have."

BACK TO CALIFORNIA

Nixon pointed to the pad of paper on his desk and said he was writing out notes for a speech to announce he wouldn't run. "No, you must do whatever you think is right," Pat said.[6] So on September 27 in Los Angeles, Nixon announced that he would not run for president in 1964 but instead would run for governor in 1962.

Before Nixon could even face Brown in the main election, he had to win the Republican primary. The problem was that even though he had been the Republican choice for president little more than a year before, he was not the unanimous Republican choice for governor of California.

Southern California was a hotbed of support for the right-wing John Birch Society, and many right-wingers preferred Joseph Shell, the GOP leader of the state Assembly. Some Birchers had accused even Eisenhower and his secretary of state, John Foster Dulles, of being Communists. Nixon had to refute such statements and refused to appear on any platform with members of the John Birch Society. Nixon managed to defeat Shell easily in the primary, but in the process he lost the support of many Republicans, several of whom were heavy contributors to political campaigns.

Back on the campaign trail with Nixon were many aides and advisers who had helped him campaign in 1960: men like Bob Haldeman, John Ehrlichman, and Bob Finch. They were something of a collection of yes-men, always agreeing with orders from Nixon, whom they called "RN" or "The Boss."

Nixon found that many of the California newspapers, some of them very sympathetic to him in past campaigns, were now making a strong effort not to look as if they favored him. They wanted to be fair to both candidates. In the *Los Angeles Times* equal-size articles had to be written about both Nixon and Brown, both sides of the story had to be told. But Nixon didn't see it that way; he began to suspect a conspiracy. "He was neo-paranoid about the press," said William Bagley, then a California assemblyman who traveled with Nixon during the campaign to advise him about California issues.[7] One of Bagley's jobs was to keep a chief political writer from the *Los Angeles Times* away from Nixon, an almost impossible task.

The press, in turn, liked to needle Nixon. On one ride on a campaign bus, Nixon was sitting in front while a dozen or more reporters sat in back. The reporters began singing the letters of his name to the Mickey Mouse Club theme song: "R-I-C-H-A-R-D N-I-X-O-N." Nixon turned around, scowled, and then laughed, trying to show he was taking it in good humor, but hostility ran just below the surface on both sides.

Pat Brown's chief weapon against Nixon was the charge that Nixon was using the state of California as a stepping-stone to the White House, and the press often echoed this allegation. Nixon would try to talk to the press about his proposals for California, and then the reporters started asking him questions about national and international issues, questions which he would feel forced to answer. "Most reporters showed little interest in the many detailed proposals I made on the cost of state government, crime, education, or the necessity for creating a better business climate in California," he said.[8]

A fair number of dirty tricks were played by candidates on both sides. The Democrats planted their spies inside the Nixon camp, and the Republicans had theirs following the Democrats. One night when the Brown campaigners were staging a telephone blitz to Democrats to urge them to get out to vote, the Nixon campaign staff got rolls of dimes and ran from pay phone to pay phone dialing the Brown telephones to try to tie up the lines.

The Nixon campaign accused Brown of being soft on Communism and printed up bumper stickers saying, "Is Brown Pink?" Meanwhile, the Brown staff accused Nixon of being a racist because of a covenant he had signed on a house he had bought in Washington in 1951. The fine print of the deed said that homes in the neighborhood could not be sold to Jews or blacks. Nixon did not respond to the charge because he would have had to confess he hadn't read all the papers when he bought the house.

A more serious charge for Nixon involved billionaire

Howard Hughes. Several years before, Nixon's brother Donald had borrowed $205,000 from the Hughes Tool Company, a government defense contractor. Nixon's mother had put up a piece of property as security. The Democrats charged that Hughes made the loan in order to get a favorable ruling from the government on a tax matter. In fact, Donald Nixon was never able to repay the loan. Nixon contended that he had no role in the loan and noted that his mother had eventually signed the property over to Hughes. During the campaign, Nixon said, he must have answered questions about the Hughes loan at least a hundred times.

As the polls began to show that Brown was ahead, Nixon grew increasingly weary of the campaign. One day he toured a fish-packing plant in San Pedro, in southern California. It was a dreary visit, according to William Bagley, because clearly 95 percent of the workers intended to vote for Brown. Nixon went up and down the assembly line, where tuna and crab were moving along a conveyor belt. The workers tried to get their rubber gloves off in order to shake his hand. When he got back on the freeway to head to his next campaign stop, there was total silence in the Nixon car. Suddenly, without a word of preface, Nixon turned around and told Bagley, "Bill, the lesson here is never go on television to debate someone when you're tired."[9] Everyone in the car knew Nixon was referring to his infamous first debate with John F. Kennedy and the devastating effect it had had on his presidential campaign.

The final blow came on October 22 when President Kennedy announced that the Russians had moved nuclear missiles into Cuba and that in response the United States had imposed a naval blockade of Cuba. Kennedy demanded that Khrushchev remove the missiles. While the whole world, fearing the outbreak of nuclear war, waited for the Soviet reply, the California gubernatorial campaign was pushed to the back pages of the newspaper. Nixon believed he had to stand behind Kennedy and support his action.

On top of it all, the night before the election, Nixon held a telethon with his wife and daughters and made a serious flub. He began answering a question by saying he was running for "Governor of the United States." Brown quickly pounced on the error.

Nixon went to the polls that November knowing that he had no chance of winning. His instincts had been right; it was a mistake to try to run for governor of California. On Election Day, his daughter Tricia wrote in her diary: "Today was the second saddest day of my life, the first being the 1960 Presidential election. Last night, election eve, the greatest man in the United States of America told his family that it would be a miracle if he won the election for governor of California."[10] In the end he lost to Brown by 297,000 votes out of a total of 6 million.

The next morning, after a night of almost no sleep in a Los Angeles hotel, he watched on television while reporters harassed his aide Herb Klein, who was reading his concession speech in the hotel ballroom. Growing steadily more angry, Nixon marched downstairs to give his statement in person to reporters.

There are varying accounts of what he looked like that morning. John Ehrlichman contends that Nixon had been drinking the night before and was red-eyed and hung over. Nixon himself said he had not had time to shave and looked and felt terrible. But photographs indicate that aside from looking tired, he did not look disheveled and wore a well-pressed business suit.

Standing at the podium, Nixon waved his fist and launched into a rambling statement. First, he thanked his campaign workers; then he began talking about the press. He said that never in sixteen years of campaigning had he ever complained to a publisher or editor about a writer. "I believe a reporter has got a right to write it as he feels it," he said. But still, he said, for sixteen years, ever since the Hiss case, reporters had had fun attacking him. "But as I leave you I want you to know—just think how much you're going to be missing. You won't have Nixon to kick around anymore, because, gentlemen, this is my last press conference. . . ."[11]

As Nixon stepped away from the microphones, his staff

was stunned. He had let his emotions show in a way considered taboo in American politics; he had attacked the press openly, a group that was unlikely to forgive this outburst. His enemies were gleeful. Columnists and commentators prepared to tear him apart. Nixon had been trounced in his home state, and he had admitted he was finished.

When Nixon arrived home, his tearful wife and daughters were waiting at the front door. He brushed past them and went out into the backyard.

"That afternoon was the first, and the only, time my parents gave way to their emotions simultaneously," said Julie Nixon Eisenhower, "and it bewildered Tricia and me."[12] In a darkened bedroom, Pat lay on the bed sobbing, and Tricia and Julie sat on the floor and cried.

Not long after the election, ABC television carried a half-hour news special, *The Political Obituary of Richard Nixon.* Among those asked to comment on Nixon's defeats was Alger Hiss, whom Nixon once helped put into prison. But soon hundreds of angry callers barraged the station with complaints about the program. Thousands of letters poured in saying that the program had been in bad taste. Nixon still had friends left in the world despite the disastrous campaign for governor.

A few days later, Nixon drove his still grieving daughters to school. As Tricia left the car, he stopped her to give her some encouraging words: "In life, you don't always win and it's difficult to lose, but you just go on. You go on with your head high."[13]

CHAPTER TEN

HEALING THE WOUNDS

T H E loss in California left deep scars, and suddenly the Nixons no longer wanted to live in their home state anymore. Nixon was interested in moving to New York to practice law with a large firm. Pat Nixon liked the idea. If they moved to New York, he wouldn't run for office anymore, she thought.

In the spring of 1963, Nixon joined a New York firm which changed its name to Nixon, Mudge, Rose, Guthrie and Alexander when he became a partner. The family bought a ten-room cooperative apartment, and the girls were enrolled in a private school in New York City. With his new legal job, his investments, and his book royalties, Nixon's annual income soon rose to $200,000. During his years in New York, Nixon also made real estate investments in Florida with his friend Bebe Rebozo.

Because of his friendships among big businessmen, Nixon brought many lucrative accounts to the firm, including Pepsi-Cola and the Precision Valve Corporation.

As a lawyer Nixon even tried a case before the Supreme Court. His clients were the James Hill family of Philadelphia, who had been held prisoner in their home for nineteen hours by escaped convicts. *Life* magazine later ran a story about a Broadway play that depicted their ordeal, and they sued for invasion of privacy. Nixon prepared thoroughly for the case, but the high court ruled five to four that freedom of the press superceded the right to privacy.

In late November 1963, Nixon was riding home from the airport in a taxicab when he heard that John F. Kennedy had been shot during a presidential trip to Dallas. Nixon sat up late into the night in his library thinking about his feelings about Kennedy and the bitterness of the 1960 election.

He wrote to Jacqueline Kennedy, expressing his sympathy, and she wrote back. Nixon later said, "I never felt the 'there but for the grace of God go I' reaction to Kennedy's death that many people seemed to imagine I would."[1]

Soon after Kennedy's death, Arizona Senator Barry Goldwater began his drive to win the Republican nomination for president with the backing of right-wing forces in the Republican Party. But it was clear he would have a strong opponent in the presidential race in the new president, former vice president Lyndon Baines Johnson, who succeeded Kennedy in the White House.

Many moderate Republicans found Goldwater objectionable and supported other candidates, Governor William Scranton of Pennsylvania, Governor Nelson Rockefeller of New York, or Henry Cabot Lodge, Nixon's former running mate. Well-known Republicans pleaded with Nixon to run. But foreseeing a bitter fight between the two wings of his party, Nixon refused and also decided not to endorse anyone before the convention.

After Goldwater was nominated on the first ballot at the San Francisco Cow Palace, Nixon asked for the chance to present the nominee to the convention on the final night. Nixon wanted to give a speech that would unite the delegates behind Goldwater in spite of their political differences. He told the crowd:

Before this convention, we were Goldwater Republicans, Rockefeller Republicans, Scranton Republicans, Lodge Republicans. But now that this convention has met and made its decision, we are Republicans, period, working for Barry Goldwater for President of the United States.[2]

Next, Goldwater took center stage, but he spoke defiantly and harshly: "Anyone who joins us in all sincerity we welcome. Though those who don't care for our cause, we don't expect to enter our ranks in any case." The delegates who had backed other candidates were stunned as he attacked moderates of all political parties: "Extremism in the defense of liberty is no vice! . . . Moderation in the pursuit of justice is no virtue!"[3]

Those phrases were used scornfully by the Democrats throughout the presidential campaign. Over and over again, Lyndon Johnson called Goldwater an extremist. Many Republican candidates for state and local posts around the country were faced with the choice of publicly rejecting Goldwater and his ideas or endorsing him and losing.

Although Nixon was upset by Goldwater and the split in the Republican Party, he tried to act as a bridge to keep the campaign from becoming a total disaster. He arranged a summit meeting of Republican leaders to show that they had made peace. He traveled the country for five weeks campaigning for friends and made 150 appearances. Although it did little good, it won him many political friends. He stood by the Republican Party and its presidential ticket when many others were deserting it.

On November 3, 1963, Johnson won by a landslide. Not only was Goldwater badly beaten; so were many other Republicans. The GOP lost thirty-seven seats in the House of Representatives, two in the Senate, and more than 500 in state legislatures.

To many, it seemed that the Republican Party was finished. But Nixon wasn't crushed by the loss; he saw it as a chance for him to step in and bring the party together. Nixon also began to think about running for president again in 1968. He thought that Lyndon Johnson was sure to start running into problems with his own party and with the press.

He didn't tell his family all this because he knew Pat and his daughters would be upset. "But I had finally come to the realization that there was no other life for me but politics and public service. Even when my legal work was at its most interesting I never found it truly fulfilling," he said.[4]

After his election, Lyndon Johnson pushed for heavy government spending to finance the social programs that he labeled the Great Society. Johnson wanted to carry on the reforms of President Franklin D. Roosevelt's New Deal; he wanted to feed the hungry and shelter the homeless and educate the poor.

But by 1965, he faced a foreign-policy crisis that threatened to sidetrack those programs—the war in Vietnam. Both Kennedy and Johnson had been drawn deeper and deeper into the quagmire in Vietnam. Under President Kennedy, the number of American soldiers advising the Vietnamese about their war had grown to 16,000. American pilots had secretly begun to fly combat missions out of Saigon; the United States began to ship helicopters to Vietnam.

Johnson wanted his Great Society, but he did not want to be known as the president who had lost Vietnam and possibly all of Southeast Asia to the Communists. Although some advisers told him the United States should pull out before it was too late, he kept sending men and equipment into Vietnam.

In August 1964, Johnson had sent the first American pilots over North Vietnam in bombing missions designed to punish the North Vietnamese for harassing an American destroyer in the Tonkin Gulf off North Vietnam. In July 1965, the first American combat troops were sent to Vietnam. By 1966, there were more than 300,000 Americans there.

Few in Congress or the rest of the country objected to all this. Nixon, who visited Vietnam in 1964 and 1965, believed that Johnson was too restrained in the war effort. He also believed that Johnson should have told the public how serious the conflict in Vietnam really was. "The country should have been informed of how difficult and costly the struggle would be," Nixon said.[5]

Nixon thought that if the United States allowed South Vietnam to fall, all of Asia could be taken over by the Communists. During 1965, he made speeches about Vietnam and urged that the United States bomb the Communists' supply routes and hideouts in North Vietnam and Laos. However, he opposed sending more troops to Vietnam, and instead wanted fuller use of American air and sea power.

Between the 1964 presidential election and the 1966 congressional elections, Nixon traveled to forty states and spoke to 400 groups. He was a highly successful fund-raiser for the Republicans, bringing in more than $4 million.

Despite Pat's opposition to his return to politics, she began helping in his office by answering phone calls and political letters. But she refused to go on his fund-raising trips. Tricia and Julie were by then in college, Tricia at Hunter College in New York City and Julie at Smith College in Massachusetts.

As the fall 1966 campaign took shape, Nixon visited thirty-five states on behalf of Republican candidates. Many of his messages attacked President Johnson's financial policies. "Every time a housewife goes into a supermarket today, she is faced with the High Cost of Johnson," he told his audiences.[6]

At the end of the 1966 campaign, Nixon scored a political blow against Johnson that won him new respect from the press. It came about when Johnson made a trip to the Philippines to meet with South Vietnamese leaders and other Asian allies in Vietnam. The group made some diplomatic proposals that Nixon objected to, and he wrote a statement on the theme he had stressed for months—that Johnson did not need to send soldiers to Vietnam, he just had to increase bombing and naval raids. He criticized Johnson on the one hand for not committing enough military effort to the war, but on the other for rapidly raising the number of Americans fighting in Vietnam. "How many more American troops—in addition to this latest 46,000— do we currently plan to send to fight in Vietnam in 1967?" he asked.[7]

Nixon was not a public official, he was just a campaigner for other politicians. His statement was typical campaign rhetoric. But Nixon's political aides talked the *New York Times* into printing it. That in itself was a victory. Then

President Johnson lashed out at Nixon and called him a "chronic campaigner" who "never realized what was going on even when he had an official office."[8]

For Nixon, it was a lucky break. Suddenly the press and the president were taking him seriously again. He could afford to respond graciously, and he was relaxed and confident when he talked to reporters about Johnson. "Now President Johnson and I can disagree . . . but let's disagree as gentlemen," he told one reporter. "Let's disagree as men who are trying to find the right way."[9]

The man whose "last" press conference had revealed the worst about his personality was suddenly at ease under attack by a president whose nerves seemed frayed over an international crisis. Nixon was looking and acting presidential.

To top it off, the Republicans scored heavily in the November elections, winning forty-seven more seats in the House of Representatives, three more seats in the Senate, and eight more governors' posts. Nixon was viewed as an important key to the comeback for the Republicans. His planning could begin in earnest for the 1968 Republican presidential nomination.

There were other candidates in the wings, of course— George Romney, Ronald Reagan, Nelson Rockefeller, and even Goldwater—but Nixon wanted to remain officially undecided for a while. Although the first Nixon for President committee was formed and Nixon began to hire political aides, he took a six-month vacation from politics and made visits to Europe, the Soviet Union, Latin America, Africa and the Middle East, and of course Vietnam.

By Christmas 1967, Nixon knew he had to make a decision about whether to run. Vietnam was causing increasing upheaval in the Democratic Party, and he believed that chances looked good for a Republican candidate. Political polls indicated that Nixon might beat Johnson. But still some of Nixon's supporters had doubts about his running again.

One evening after a Christmas party, Nixon sat down in front of the fire in his study and listed reasons why he should not become a candidate, everything from the pain that losing caused his family to his exhaustion with asking political and business friends for support once again. At the bottom of the page, he even wrote: "I don't give a damn."[10]

For the next few weeks, Nixon debated the idea and asked friends and relatives for advice. On January 9, his fifty-fifth birthday, he made up his mind: he would run. He waited to tell his family until a dinner party when his girls were home from school and Rose Mary Woods, his faithful secretary, was there.

He covered the pros and cons with his family, but said he was going to try again—and this time he would win. There were cheers and toasts, but Pat was grave and subdued. "Now that the decision is made," she said, "I will go along with it."[11]

CHAPTER ELEVEN

THE "NEW" NIXON

N I X O N and his staff planned carefully for his entry into the 1968 primaries, beginning with the New Hampshire election in March. The key to the race, they decided, was giving Richard Nixon a new image as a man who was relaxed and confident, a man who could sometimes laugh at himself, and a man who could win.

Was he really a different person? Many people found him more mature, more honest, more cheerful. But the real truth, says William Safire, a speechwriter for Nixon, was that Nixon was always a man with many layers of personality. On the surface he could be icy, arrogant, and aloof, but he was also sometimes impulsive and sentimental: one of the few knickknacks on his desk was a china Irish setter he had given to Pat during their courtship days.

Although conservatives saw him as a tough, gutsy self-made man who told the rest of the world to stand on its own two feet just as he had, he was also a progressive politician at heart, with views on domestic issues that were middle of the road and sometimes left of center, Safire says. He was a man of courage and determination, but he was also a man who trampled on the civil rights of others when angry and upset.

"That's the trouble with most perceptions of Nixon," Safire says. "One layer or another is chosen as 'real' and the perceiver roots for that one layer's success. But the whole cake is the 'real' Nixon."[1]

In organizing the 1968 campaign, Nixon staff member H. R. Haldeman wanted Nixon to use television in new, dynamic ways to win votes. Traveling from rally to rally, meeting to meeting, to speak to a few thousand people at a time burned up days and weeks. But on television a candidate reached millions in a single moment.

Several candidates looked like strong opponents for Nixon in early 1968, but the toughest seemed to be George Romney, the governor of Michigan, who had scored strongly in the political opinion polls. Romney also had the backing of New York's governor, Nelson Rockefeller.

But the press zeroed in on Romney and criticized his fuzzy statements on national and international problems. Then came the biggest blunder of all. Romney was interviewed on television and asked why he had once endorsed the Vietnam War. He said that during a trip to Vietnam, he had undergone "brainwashing" by the U.S. generals and diplomats.[2] The press pounced on this single sentence which seemed to indicate that Romney was incapable of making up his own mind. The generals and diplomats were furious. Very quickly, Romney's campaign sputtered and fell apart. On February 28, Romney bowed out.

Meanwhile, on the Democratic side, the subject of the Vietnam War was creating upheaval as well. President Johnson poured men and equipment into Vietnam while American generals told the press that the United States and its ally South Vietnam were winning the war against the Communist Vietcong.

But on January 31, 1968, 70,000 Communist soldiers launched a surprise attack during Tet, the lunar New Year holiday, when they had pledged a cease-fire. City after city in Vietnam was rocked by conflict in which American soldiers were dying, and at home, troubled Americans watched it all on television news shows. A group of commandos actually managed to invade the fortresslike U.S. embassy in Saigon, the capital of South Vietnam. Although American soldiers and the South Vietnamese quickly crushed the attacks, more and more Americans believed the war in Vietnam might never end.

A group known as the National Conference of Concerned Democrats, largely liberal politicians and college students, tried to find a candidate to oppose Johnson in the primaries. John F. Kennedy's brother Robert, a senator from New York, turned them down, but Senator Eugene McCarthy of Minnesota agreed to run. McCarthy launched a barebones, shoestring campaign in New Hampshire with a staff of Ivy League college students. Predictions were that he would poll only a few percentage points on the Democratic ballot.

Nixon was often asked what he would do to end the war, but he declined to give details even though he felt that Johnson was not handling the war properly. "I believed that we could use our armed strength more effectively to convince the North Vietnamese that a military victory was not possible," he said. ". . . Most important, I believed that we were not making adequate use of our vast diplomatic resources and powers. The heart of the problem lay more in Peking and Moscow than in Hanoi."[3]

On Election Day in New Hampshire, March 12, Nixon polled 78 percent of the vote in the Republican primary—a significant win that showed other Republicans and the press that his losing days were over. In the Democratic primary, Johnson managed to beat McCarthy, but by only a slim margin, 49.5 percent of the vote versus 42.4 percent. Although Johnson had won, the size of McCarthy's vote impressed the press and other politicians.

By the end of March, Nixon was ready to deliver a nationwide radio speech on Vietnam. He planned to propose that the United States get the Soviet Union to cut back military aid to North Vietnam. He asked for radio time on the evening of March 31 but could not get it because Johnson had scheduled a presidential address for the same time. Johnson's speech turned out to be the surprise announcement that he would not seek the nomination for another term as president. Nixon's speech was never given.

In the next primary, in Wisconsin on April 2, Nixon won again, and McCarthy had a landslide victory against Johnson, who was no longer in the race. But other candidates were waiting in the wings. Vice President Hubert Humphrey and Robert Kennedy entered the campaign for the Democratic nomination.

Former governor George Wallace of Alabama, meanwhile, bolted the Democratic Party to form a conservative-based third party. In the past many of his appeals had had a racist message. It was believed that he would be more of a threat to the Republicans than to the Democrats because he would pull votes of Southerners who were thinking of switching to the Republican Party.

Nixon also faced new opposition. In California, Governor Ronald Reagan had decided to become a favorite-son candidate in a primary that Nixon decided not to enter. In April, New York's Nelson Rockefeller also decided to run for the Republican nomination. But Rockefeller didn't seem like a very serious candidate. He was too late to get his name into the primaries.

So Nixon kept rolling along scoring victories, virtually unopposed. In a way, the Republican primaries seemed almost boring compared to the Democratic races and their battling candidates. But as historian Theodore H. White noted: "Millions of Americans in their year of stress wanted precisely that, an 'unexciting' Presidency, a calm and soothing regime which would not prod them with the increasing perplexities of America and the world."[4]

Nixon built a smoothly operating campaign staff including many who would someday hold jobs in the White House. On top was John Mitchell, a member of Nixon's former law firm. Other key people were Herbert Klein, Ronald Ziegler, and Richard Kleindienst. H. R. Haldeman was the chief of Nixon's personal staff, assisted by Dwight Chapin. Nixon's ever-loyal secretary, Rose Mary Woods, also worked closely with him during the campaign. Another key person, with no official title, was Robert Finch, lieutenant governor of California.

According to Haldeman, the 1968 campaign was moving much more smoothly than the one in 1960. "In 1960 we ran it badly and he [Nixon] was always angry with the need of dealing with petty details that were handled badly," Haldeman said. "He has no time for small talk or the ordinary kind of bull when people sit down together. He's best when he's dealing with problems—you have to keep people off his back."[5]

Two days after the Wisconsin primary, politicking was halted after civil rights leader Martin Luther King, Jr. was assassinated in Memphis, Tennessee. Nixon's advisers debated whether he should go to the funeral, whether it would look like a grandstand play for black votes. In the end he flew to Atlanta to visit the King family and attend the funeral, but he did not march in the funeral parade.

Hours after King's death, the nation's big cities were rocked by riots and protests in black neighborhoods. More than 50,000 federal and National Guard troops were called in to stop the bloodshed.

That spring as well, campuses around the country were hit by violent student demonstrations and strikes. Sometimes students protested racial discrimination or university rules; sometimes the turmoil focused on Vietnam.

Two months later, the nation was shaken again when Robert Kennedy was assassinated after winning the primary in California. "With millions of other Americans I thought, how could such ghastly tragedy be revisited on the Kennedy family? . . . When would this madness come to an end?" Nixon later wrote.[6]

Security was tightened for all the candidates. Nixon had to move out of his office in a New York building because Secret Service men told him he would be too easy a target for a sharpshooter aiming at his window from a building nearby.

Finally, in early August, the Republican National Convention opened in Miami Beach. Although Nixon seemed to have sewed up the nomination (he was polishing his acceptance speech), Rockefeller and Reagan kept telling delegates that Nixon was losing support.

Nixon's convention headquarters was the top four stories of the Hilton-Plaza where 200 rooms buzzed with activity. Nixon was confident that he held leads among delegates from all parts of the country except the Northeast, where Rockefeller was strong. There was little conflict as the various forces drew up the campaign platform. All contributed to the resolution on Vietnam, but there was nothing in the way of new solutions to the war. Basically, the Republicans said they supported a positive program for peace in Vietnam and wanted to develop a clear negotiating position.

Balloting began on Thursday morning, August 8, and one by one the states fell the way that Nixon had expected. In the end Richard Nixon racked up 692 votes, Nelson Rockefeller 277, and Ronald Reagan 182. Yet Nixon had won on the first ballot by only twenty-five more than the necessary 667-vote majority.

Rockefeller soon phoned Nixon to give his congratulations. "Your strategy was perfect," he told him. "You handled it perfectly."[7]

After that, Nixon and his advisers huddled to choose his running mate. Name after name was suggested: Senator Charles Percy of Illinois, New York's mayor John Lindsay, California governor Ronald Reagan, Oregon senator Mark Hatfield, Senator John Tower of Texas. Nixon wanted his close friend Robert Finch of California, but Finch refused. And there were a few new names as well, like Spiro Agnew, the governor of Maryland, who had placed Nixon's name in nomination a few hours before. Agnew was known as a moderate and before the convention had leaned toward Rockefeller.

The Republicans from Southern states didn't want a liberal like Lindsay or Percy or Hatfield; the Northerners didn't want a conservative like Reagan or Tower.

Finally, early Thursday afternoon, Nixon decided; he

chose Agnew, a virtual unknown to most Americans. "Absolute shock and surprise greeted my announcement," he later noted.[8]

That evening in the convention hall, the crowd roared its approval as Nixon and Agnew took the platform. Nixon was onstage with his arms thrust up in the air, his fingers wiggling in his trademark *V* symbol. Then he began his speech, one which many said was among the best he ever gave. He sounded a call to all those Americans worried about the unrest over Vietnam, the riots in the ghettos and on the campuses. But he also talked to those who wanted to reach out to the disadvantaged:

> *I see a day when Americans are once again proud of their flag. I see a day when the President of the United States is respected. . . . I see a day when every child in this land, regardless of his background, has a chance for the best education our wisdom and schools can provide. . . .*[9]

He also sounded a theme he would repeat again and again, an appeal to the many Americans who were not part of any political pressure group or lobby:

> *It is a quiet voice in the tumult of the shouting. It is the voice of the great majority of Americans, the forgotten Americans, the non-shouters, the non-demonstrators. . . . They work in American factories, they run American businesses. They serve in government; they provide most of the soldiers who die to keep it free. They give drive to the spirit of America.*[10]

He also talked about himself, about his father and mother and football coach and the others who had helped him reach his dreams.

Once the shouting ended, Nixon stepped back to see what the Democrats would do at their convention. What happened was one of the most bitter political conventions of all time, a convention stained with violence and blood. The Democrats met in Chicago, where Mayor Richard Daley had set up a system of very tight security for the Convention Hall. Antiwar demonstrators had announced that they would disrupt the convention, and Daley was determined to prevent that.

As the delegates met, Vice President Hubert Humphrey held the lead for the nomination, but thousands of young people hadn't given up on Eugene McCarthy. Still, McCarthy seemed unable to organize his drive for the presidency. He seemed to be stepping back, unsure of what he wanted to do next but unwilling to desert those who had brought him to Chicago.

Humphrey seemed weak and ineffective as well, unable to break with the Vietnam policies of Lyndon Johnson even though Humphrey did not agree with them. In the end, Humphrey agreed to a party plank on Vietnam that echoed the views of Johnson.

There were last-minute attempts to try to nominate Edward Kennedy, Bobby's and John's brother; there were scuffles among delegates on the convention floor. But most dramatic of all, the police and thousands of hippies, crazies, and legitimate peace protesters were clashing on the streets of Chicago.

As American television viewers watched Hubert Humphrey being nominated, the networks also showed shots of the mob on Michigan Avenue in Chicago shouting "The Whole World Is Watching" and "Peace Now." Angry police charged in with tear gas and clubs to break up the crowd, and somehow it seemed as if the Democrats had caused the riots.

One bright spot for Humphrey: the next day he chose Senator Edmund Muskie of Maine for his running mate, a solid, well liked, hardworking politician. In his acceptance speech, Humphrey called for a turning away from violence and hatred, but even the next day there were confrontations with the police.

A few days after the Democratic convention, Nixon had a

motorcade through downtown Chicago at noon. A half million people lined the parade route, cheering and shouting in sharp contrast with the events of a week before. The campaign had begun, and Nixon was clearly in the lead. America was learning to like the "new Nixon."

A NARROW VICTORY

E A R L Y polls after the Democratic convention showed Nixon leading Humphrey 43 percent to 31 percent.

While Humphrey faced boos and protests at his campaign stops, cheering crowds greeted Nixon in New York, Houston, and San Francisco. Not only that, while Humphrey's campaign was disorganized and sputtering, Nixon's was running strong, operating from offices on New York's Park Avenue. Humphrey was short on money, crucial in the age of television when millions are needed to buy air time. Meanwhile, Nixon had raised and spent $8 million on getting the nomination and would raise another $20 million more for his election campaign.[1]

One fear that Nixon and his staff had was that Alabama governor George Wallace might serve as a spoiler in the race, getting so many conservative votes that Nixon would win only a plurality and not a majority. In that case, the House of Representatives would choose the president, and since Democrats held the majority in the House, it was unlikely they would pick Nixon. Nixon wanted to hold down the Wallace vote without taking any of Wallace's extreme right-wing positions.

As September ended, Humphrey began to change his public stand on Vietnam. On September 30, in Salt Lake City, he said he was ready to "stop the bombing of North Vietnam as an acceptable risk for peace because I believe it could lead to success in the negotiations and thereby shorten the war."[2] It was only a slight change in his statements. Until then the Democrats had said that if the bombing were halted, the North Vietnamese must respond with some positive act.

But for Humphrey, the speech showed he did not agree completely with Lyndon Johnson anymore, and it marked a turning point in his campaign. Many Democrats decided they preferred Humphrey over Nixon in spite of the upheaval of the Democratic Convention. They may not have agreed with what went on in Chicago, but if they wanted victory in November, they had to start supporting Humphrey with work and money. Soon the hecklers disappeared from Humphrey's rallies, and instead protesters began showing up at Nixon's campaign stops.

Repeatedly, Humphrey asked Nixon to debate him on television. But Nixon, perhaps remembering the 1960 face-off with Kennedy, refused. He led Humphrey in the polls, why should he give his opponent the chance to make inroads? Humphrey responded by calling him "Richard the Chicken-Hearted," "Richard the Silent," "Richard the Last."[3]

But even though Nixon did not want to debate with Humphrey on television, he was using television as no presidential candidate had ever done before. "America still saw him as the 1960 Nixon," said Joe McGinnis in a book about the campaign. "If he were to come at the people again, as candidate, it would have to be as something new; not this scarred, discarded figure from their past."[4]

The best way to show off the new Nixon was on television. The format for his television appearances was a sort of live staged press conference, for which his staff chose a panel of seven or eight people to ask him questions for about an hour. The questioners included people from various walks of life and ethnic groups, for example, an attorney, a housewife, a businessman, a farmer, a couple of reporters, some union members. The session was telecast in front of a studio audience sympathetic to Nixon.

Although the event was staged and the press was barred from the studio during the telecasts, the panelists could ask whatever questions they wanted. The effort was to make Nixon look honest and genuine and likable. Ten of these programs were produced in states across the country during the campaign.

As October wore on, Nixon's staff knew that he was slipping in the polls. The press kept pressuring him to give more details on his plans and programs. Reporters also zeroed in on the vice-presidential candidate, Spiro Agnew, who had done serious damage to the campaign by making some racist remarks. Agnew also labeled Humphrey as "soft on Communism"; at one point he also quipped, "If you've seen one city slum, you've seen them all."[5] Meanwhile, Humphrey's running mate, Muskie, was impressing reporters with his presidential style.

Then at the last minute in the campaign, President Johnson took a bold action that almost boosted Humphrey over the edge to victory.

On October 31, Nixon was at home working on a campaign speech when Lyndon Johnson phoned. Via a special conference line, Johnson was also speaking simultaneously to the other presidential candidates, Humphrey and Wallace.

Because of a breakthrough in peace talks in Paris, he told the three men, he was halting the bombing over North Vietnam. All the candidates agreed that they supported Johnson's action, but Nixon was inwardly furious. He had heard rumors that Johnson might take this step, and Nixon believed it was motivated more by a desire to help Humphrey than to achieve peace in Vietnam.

Last-minute support surged for Humphrey among voters who thought that the end of the war might be approaching, but then the South Vietnamese announced that they would not join peace talks. The nation was in turmoil and uproar, said historian Theodore White: "On Friday morning, Americans were convinced that peace was at hand; on Saturday, Saigon's repudiation of peace upset them; by Sunday, no one knew what was happening."[6]

Nixon was also worried when Humphrey began a final blitz of television commercials. Political pollsters claimed that by then Nixon was only a percentage point or two ahead of Humphrey. In response, Nixon held a four-hour telethon the day before the election and answered questions phoned in from around the country.

On Election Day, the Nixons flew to New York City from the West Coast and checked into a suite in the Waldorf Towers. At about nine, Nixon began checking election results, but he refused to watch the television coverage himself. As the vote counting began, the totals at first went the way everyone had first expected. Nixon led in such solid Republican states as Kansas and was several points ahead in the popular vote.

But as the votes piled up, the television news people said that several states looked too close to call. By ten-thirty, the two candidates were neck and neck in the popular vote. By midnight, Humphrey led the popular count.

Nixon and his advisers waited nervously for the outcome in several key states—Illinois, California, Ohio, Missouri, and Texas—the same states that had decided the election in 1960. As the minutes ticked away, Nixon sat tensely in his suite. He talked to his staff and added up numbers on a note pad as they were relayed to him from a television monitoring room.

By 3:00 A.M. Nixon grew confident: Ohio and California were his, he had a substantial lead in Illinois, Missouri leaned his way. But still the final votes had not come in from several important states. At 5:00 A.M., Nixon's staff persuaded him to go to bed for a nap; he had been awake for almost twenty-two hours. But he couldn't sleep and soon got up again. Finally at midmorning, the cheers began; the networks had declared him the winner and new president.

Nixon's margin of victory in the popular vote was less than 500,000 votes, but it was about four times more than the margin by which he had lost to John F. Kennedy in 1960.

After Humphrey had called him to concede defeat, Nixon went down to the hotel ballroom to greet his supporters. He told them about a teenager he had seen on the campaign trail in Ohio and a sign she carried that read: BRING US TOGETHER.

"That will be the great objective of this administration at the outset," he said, "to bring the American people together."[7]

Next, Nixon began to make his Cabinet and staff appointments. H. R. Haldeman and John Ehrlichman, who had played big roles in the presidential campaign, were to have key jobs in the Nixon White House. Haldeman became Nixon's chief of staff, and Ehrlichman the president's assistant for domestic affairs. Their power in the White House would be enormous and also controversial.

William Rogers was to be secretary of state, and Melvin Laird secretary of defense. Nixon's former law partner John Mitchell was named attorney general. Henry Kissinger, a Harvard professor who had once been an adviser to Nelson Rockefeller, Nixon's rival, was to become the president's national security adviser. Charles Colson became special counsel to the president.

In the last few weeks before Nixon's inauguration, there was an important family event. Julie Nixon married David Eisenhower, the grandson of Dwight Eisenhower, during whose presidency Nixon had served as vice president. It was a happy moment for Nixon but also one tinged with sadness and regret. As he watched Julie and David take their vows in the Marble Collegiate Church in New York City, the man who had put his political career above almost everything in his life "couldn't help wondering if it would not have been possible to have spent even a little more time with her."[8]

CHAPTER THIRTEEN

FINALLY, THE WHITE HOUSE

O N January 20, 1969, Richard Milhous Nixon finally attained the goal he had sought for so many years: he was sworn in as president of the United States. He took the oath of office while holding one hand on the two Milhous family Bibles opened to a verse that talked about peace, Isaiah 2:4: "They shall beat their swords into plowshares."[1]

In his inaugural address, Nixon also talked about the peace that the nation sought in Vietnam. But when he left the Capitol for the motorcade down Pennsylvania Avenue back to the White House, it was clear that some Americans did not view him as the peacemaker he hoped to be. Sticks, stones, and beer cans were thrown at his car while antiwar protesters raised a Vietcong flag and chanted slogans.

Already Nixon had been caught up in the most pressing question in America—what to do about the Vietnam War. The war that had been President Johnson's war was now President Nixon's war. By the time he took office, 30,000 Americans had already died in Vietnam; another 10,000 would die in 1969.

Early in 1969, Nixon and his adviser Henry Kissinger contacted the Soviet government, hoping to get the Soviets to take the lead in pressuring North Vietnam to end the war. Nixon also traveled to Europe to discuss the war with leaders there. He had hoped that the change of leadership in the United States would impress North Vietnam; it did not. Instead of drawing back, the Communist soldiers seemed to be pressing harder in Vietnam.

Soon General Earle Wheeler, the chairman of the Joint Chiefs of Staff, pushed Nixon to order the bombing of areas of Cambodia where the Communists had hideouts for their troops, and in late February, Nixon gave in. Nixon and his staff wanted the operation kept secret from the press and antiwar groups. Nixon knew the North Vietnamese would not complain publicly because they did not want to admit to the world that they were using Cambodia for a base of operations.

One reporter for the *New York Times* did discover the bombing and wrote a story about it, but the article got little attention except from Nixon and Kissinger. They were angry and believed that someone connected with the high-level staff at the White House was leaking news to the press.

Nixon contacted J. Edgar Hoover, the head of the FBI, who suggested doing background checks on people suspected of passing the confidential information to the press. Hoover also proposed placing wiretaps on their phones. From 1969 to early 1971, seventeen wiretaps were installed on the phones of thirteen government aides and four news people. It was early in his administration, but the Vietnam War and his fear of the press had quickly led Nixon to infringe on the rights and privacy of others. Nixon later admitted, "None of these wiretaps turned up any proof linking anyone in the government to a specific national security leak."[2]

When these wiretaps later became public, many people viewed them as an abuse of presidential power. Nixon defended himself by noting that high government officials, including presidents Kennedy and Johnson, had been using secret wiretaps in security matters for twenty-five years. In 1972, the Supreme Court ruled that such wiretaps must be authorized by a court if the person in question was not connected with a foreign country or its agents.

This eavesdropping on phone calls may have seemed like a small thing at the time to Nixon and Kissinger. Eventually, it led to more abuses, all damaging to Nixon, and they in turn led to the Watergate crisis.

When the new wave of bombing had little effect, Nixon's secretary of defense, Melvin Laird, proposed a new plan, "Vietnamization," calling for withdrawing some of the half million U.S. soldiers and training and equipping Vietnamese to replace them.

In early August 1969, Kissinger began secret meetings in Paris with a Communist negotiator, Xuan Thuy, but the two seemed to get nowhere. Kissinger insisted that troops on both sides must withdraw; Xuan Thuy insisted that the Saigon government in South Vietnam must disband.

The troop withdrawals and cuts in the draft calls that Nixon made during Vietnamization calmed antiwar feeling for a while. Opinion polls showed that the public had confidence in Nixon. But a storm of antiwar protests broke again as students returned to school. On October 15, 1969, the first so-called Vietnam Moratorium was held. In several cities, huge crowds met and listened to speeches by opponents of the war. The demonstrations were peaceable, and many of the listeners were older and middle class—not just bearded college students.

Nixon decided to give a major television speech on Vietnam on November 3, two weeks before another Moratorium was to be held. In his mind, the Moratorium raised the question of whether the president or Congress should allow public protests and rallies to influence their decisions. He wrote the speech himself, working at it as if it had been an inaugural address. He did twelve drafts before he was finished.

The speech told the nation that Nixon would hold firm in Vietnam. He would keep on withdrawing troops, he said, but "We are going to continue fighting until the Communists agreed to negotiate a fair and honorable peace or until the South Vietnamese were able to defend themselves on their own." In the speech, he coined the phrase "the great silent majority of Americans."[3] He asked the silent majority, those not marching in protests or sitting in on campuses, to speak out.

They responded with thousands of favorable phone calls, letters, and telegrams. Nixon felt that this wave of support bought him more time in Vietnam. He did not have to end the war immediately; the people were behind him.

Some of his aides even claimed that in two more years America might push the Communists out of South Vietnam. "If I could hold the domestic front together until then," Nixon said, "winning an honorable peace would redeem the interim difficulties."[4] Just like Lyndon Johnson, he did not want to be the first U.S. president ever to lose a war, especially not when victory might be only two years away.

While Nixon had his problems with Vietnam, his relationship with the Democratic majority in Congress was rocky as well. Some members of the Supreme Court had resigned, and the Senate rejected two judges whom Nixon chose as replacements. Both were strongly conservative Southerners and faced charges that they were racist. But the Senate did confirm four other Nixon nominees to the Supreme Court: Warren Burger as chief justice, and Harry Blackmun, Lewis Powell, and William Rehnquist as associate justices.

Nixon had many new ideas for handling domestic problems, some of them much more liberal than expected from a Republican. For example, he proposed a Family Assistance Plan designed to give federal financial help not just to the unemployed, but also to the working poor. But the plan required that everyone getting benefits, except for the old and sick and mothers of young children, must accept either work or training for work. Conservatives in Congress fought hard against the plan, and liberals did not fight hard enough on behalf of it. Eventually, only small portions of the proposal became law.

Nixon and his staff called for "the New Federalism," taking powers and funds out of the hands of bureaucrats in Washington and putting them in the hands of state and local governments. He persuaded Congress to approve his proposals for revenue sharing.

One bright spot that first year was in July, when American astronaut Neil Armstrong became the first man to walk on the moon. Nixon viewed the moon landing as a high point for a nation weary of protest marches and riots, and he participated as much as possible in the event. He talked to Armstrong via phone from the Oval Office. He also traveled to the middle of the Pacific to greet the astronauts when they splashed down.

But always the shadow of Vietnam hung over Nixon. The situation grew so difficult in the spring of 1970 that he and his wife could not attend the college graduations of Julie and her husband, David Eisenhower. Nixon feared that protesters would disrupt the ceremonies if he attended.

The secret talks between Kissinger and the Vietnamese were crawling along with no progress. Not only that, but chaos reigned in Vietnam's neighbor, Cambodia, where there had been a military coup. Communist forces moved in on the Cambodian capital of Phnom Penh. Nixon wrote a memo to Kissinger explaining that he believed U.S. forces had to step in. "They are romping in there, and the only government in Cambodia in the last twenty-five years that had the guts to take a pro-Western and pro-American stand is ready to fall," he said.[5]

In late April 1970, Nixon's military advisers recommended invading two areas of Cambodia that jutted into South Vietnam, using about 20,000 soldiers from both the South Vietnamese army and U.S. forces. Some in the Cabinet objected, but Nixon wanted to go ahead. "I recognized," he later said, "that it could mean personal and political catastrophe."[6]

The problem was that Nixon did not have the approval of Cambodia's leader, Lon Nol. In addition, some American officials questioned whether he had the power under the Constitution to invade another country without the approval of Congress.

The South Vietnamese announced the operation on April 29, and members of both houses of Congress blasted Nixon. The next night, he made a television speech in which many people felt he sounded belligerent and angry. He told Americans: "To protect our men who are in Vietnam and to guarantee the continued success of our withdrawal and Vietnamization programs, I have concluded that the time has come for action."[7]

After the speech, Nixon's political friends congratulated him but the press attacked him. The *New York Times* called the invasion a "virtual renunciation" of his promise to seek peace. State Department officials signed petitions against the action, and Nixon's secretary of the interior, Walter Hickel, objected publicly.

Meanwhile, the invasion turned into a skirmish with no heavy fighting. The North Vietnamese fled, leaving behind empty huts, although the Americans did find and destroy some enemy supplies. But Nixon kept insisting that the invasion had been one of the most successful actions of the war.

The next day, Nixon visited the Pentagon to urge officers to "blow the hell out" of the Communist sanctuaries in Cambodia.[8] He also told cheering employees in a Pentagon hallway that American soldiers were great, patriotic heroes, while at colleges "you see these bums, you know, blowing up the campuses."[9] When the "bums" remark touched off angry criticism in the press, Nixon said he was referring only to troublemaking students who used violence.

Soon there was new anger and unrest at colleges. At Kent State University in Ohio, students opposed to the war marched on the Army reserve officers training building and burned it down. National Guardsmen were called to the campus. Angered by the rock-throwing protesters, the Guardsmen opened fire and killed four students. "Those few days after Kent State were among the darkest of my presidency," Nixon said. "I felt utterly dejected when I read that the father of one of the dead girls had told a reporter, 'My child was not a bum.' "[10]

After the shocking killings, protests spread to other campuses. Four hundred and fifty colleges were shut down by striking students and professors. The National Guard was called out at twenty-one more campuses.

Henry Kissinger felt the pressure as former colleagues

from Harvard urged him to resign. Four of his aides quit and wanted him to do the same. Nixon reassured him, "Don't waste time rehashing things we can't do anything about."[11]

But Nixon was also upset. After a year and a half in the most powerful job in the world, he had done little to separate the United States from the problems of a small country thousands of miles away from Washington. His action in Cambodia did not change negotiations between North Vietnam and the United States either.

One night, after a press conference at which he tried to explain the Cambodian operation, he could not sleep. He sat in the Lincoln Sitting Room watching young people gathered on the Washington Ellipse for a National Day of Protest over what had taken place at Kent State. Suddenly, he decided to drive out to the Lincoln Memorial. His valet, Manolo Sanchez, accompanied him.

At the memorial, he jumped out of the car and walked up to the rotunda, where students had gathered. He started talking, rambling a bit, comparing his situation to that of Winston Churchill, the British prime minister who had stood firm against the Nazis during World War II. He talked about China and how he hoped to reopen that country and about other countries and their problems. He asked the students questions about their college sports teams.

One student told him, "I hope you realize that we are willing to die for what we believe in." Nixon replied, "Do you realize that many of us when we were your age were also willing to die for what we believed in?"[12]

When the sun came up, Nixon was ready to leave. As a final gesture, when he saw one of the students taking his picture, he offered to have one of his staff members snap a shot of Nixon and the student together.

This nighttime visit to the Memorial was a sentimental, impulsive gesture for which Nixon took a lot of criticism. The impression on the evening television news shows, said Nixon staff member William Safire, "was that the President, a few days after calling some students who set fire to campuses 'bums,' had compounded his error by talking condescendingly about trivial matters like football or visiting foreign cities with students who had come in seriousness to protest about the war."[13]

There were not just peaceful protests by students in 1970; there were also bombings and bomb scares by revolutionary groups on college campuses and at police stations.

In June 1970, Nixon met with officials of the Central Intelligence Agency and FBI to discuss how to cope with the violence. One official present was Tom Huston, a White House lawyer, who proposed a program of opening of mail, phone bugging and break-ins to be used against suspected terrorists. Nixon at first approved the plan and then withdrew his approval after Attorney General John Mitchell and FBI director Hoover objected to some of the proposals. Although he canceled the plan, Nixon insisted that all the methods proposed had been used may times before by the FBI and other agencies.

As the congressional elections of 1970 drew closer, Nixon at first decided not to campaign heavily; he would leave that job up to Vice President Agnew. But soon the GOP polls showed that the Republicans were in trouble and could lose up to thirty seats in the House of Representatives. So Nixon started campaigning, visiting twenty-two states in the last three weeks before the election.

Everywhere he went, crowds of demonstrators turned up. At one appearance, in San Jose, California, Nixon climbed on the hood of a car and flashed his famous V-sign at the protesters. They began throwing rocks and vegetables at him. He got into his car without being hit, but the attack triggered the same kind of knee-jerk angry response from him as his trip through Latin America had done many years before. He lashed out at the protesters in his next speech, in Phoenix, Arizona. "Let's recognize these people for what they are," he told the cheering crowd. "They are not romantic revolutionaries. They are the same thugs and hoodlums that have always plagued the good people."[14]

On November 3, the Republicans lost nine House seats and won two more in the Senate; eleven governorships were lost. But over all, Nixon was pleased with the results, which had been expected to be much more devastating for the Republicans.

The difficult election led Nixon to turn his sights on planning for his own 1972 presidential race. Nixon and his staff put little faith in the ability of the Republican National Committee to assist in his campaign for reelection. They decided to set up a separate group, the Committee to Re-Elect the President, to handle the job.

John Mitchell was chosen as the campaign manager and was to be helped by Jeb Stuart Magruder, an aide to Haldeman. Maurice Stans, secretary of commerce, became the finance chairman and chief fund-raiser for the Committee to Re-Elect the President.

Nixon wanted to get organized; he wanted to find out what the Democrats were doing. "Sometimes I ordered a tail on a front-running Democrat," he later admitted. "Sometimes I urged that department and agency files be checked for any indications of suspicious or illegal activities involving prominent Democrats."[15]

(Above) The "new" Nixon resurgent. With vice-presidential running mate Spiro T. Agnew at the 1968 Republican National Convention. (Below) Nixon's 1968 Democratic opponent, Vice President Hubert Humphrey of Minnesota.

(Above) Nixon is inaugurated president on January 20, 1969, on the steps of the Capitol, while Pat looks on. (Below) Nixon and Henry A. Kissinger, who served in the administration as national security affairs adviser and then as secretary of state.

(Above) Nixon meets U.S. troops in South Vietnam, July 1969.
(Below) Nixon jokes with *Apollo 11* astronauts (left to right) Edwin ''Buzz''
Aldrin, Michael Collins, and Neil Armstrong after their historic
1969 moon mission.

(Above) National guardsmen hurl tear gas at demonstrators on the campus of Kent State University in Ohio (1970). Four students died during the protests. (Below) American troops leaving Vietnam in 1971. "Vietnamization," or replacement of American forces by Vietnamese, was the stated policy of the Nixon administration. U.S. involvement in the war finally ended in 1973.

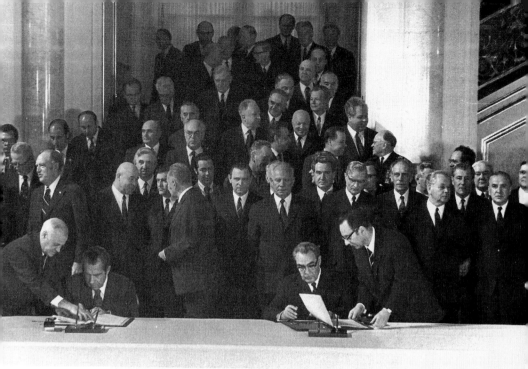

(Above) Nixon had a number of foreign policy successes. Here he signs the Strategic Arms Limitation Treaty (SALT) alongside Soviet Communist party leader Leonid Brezhnev. (Below) Nixon meets Chinese leader Mao Tse-tung during his historic 1972 visit to China.

(Above) George S. McGovern, Nixon's 1972 Democratic challenger, clenching hands with Coretta Scott King. Nixon won a landslide victory in which McGovern won only two states. (Below) The Watergate complex in Washington, D.C.

(Above) G. Gordon Liddy, a lawyer on Nixon's reelection committee, was one of the masterminds of the Watergate break-in. (Below) When it was revealed that Nixon had recorded his telephone conversations, the House Judiciary Committee subpoenaed the tapes. Nixon responded by offering edited transcripts on the grounds that the tapes contained information vital to national security.

(Above) A 1973 impeachment demonstration in Washington.
(Below) The president, second to right, meets with his Cabinet on one
of the final days of his presidency.

CHAPTER FOURTEEN

A WEEK THAT CHANGED THE WORLD

A S 1971 began, Nixon worried about his chances to be reelected president. The early months of the year seemed to be the lowest point in his first term. His ratings slipped in the opinion polls, especially compared with those of Edmund Muskie, who had been Hubert Humphrey's running mate in 1968. There were rumors, too, that Ronald Reagan would try again for the Republican nomination.

Unemployment reached 6 percent, the highest in ten years. Antiwar protests continued, and little came out of talks with the North Vietnamese. Sometimes when Kissinger met with Le Duc Tho, the chief negotiator, the atmosphere was warm and friendly and Kissinger thought a breakthrough was coming. Then at their next meeting the North Vietnamese were icy cool again.

In early 1971, Nixon and Kissinger blundered again in the Vietnam War. The two of them had expected some kind of huge Communist attack timed to influence the 1972 presidential election. Nixon's military advisers said that he could prevent this by cutting off the Ho Chi Minh Trail, a path through Laos used to transport supplies and troops to the Vietcong. The only problem was that after Nixon's last assault into Cambodia, Congress had voted to bar American ground troops from entering Cambodia or Laos. So if Nixon wanted to make a move into Laos, the operation, code-named Lamson 719, had to be run by the South Vietnamese army alone, although U.S. planes could drop bombs on the area.

Thirty thousand South Vietnamese crossed the border into Laos on February 8 and plunged into fierce fighting in which many soldiers died. They soon had to retreat, having done little if any damage to the Ho Chi Minh Trail. The attack seemed to be a defeat for Nixon's policy of Vietnamization. The South Vietnamese were unable to battle on their own.

American soldiers in Vietnam grew more and more angry and frustrated. They were bitter about lack of U.S. public support for the war. Many were draftees who did not want to be in Vietnam and did not understand why they had to stay while other soldiers were going home. An estimated 65,000 were using drugs—heroin, marijuana, speed, acid, and opium.

Suspicion and paranoia rose among the president's staff members. They had only just arrived in the White House, and already it seemed they might be losing their jobs soon because of the disastrous war in Vietnam. Top officials reacted angrily when they learned that some underlings might be leaking presidential memos to the press.

Staff members were also trying to dig up what information they could to embarrass important Democrats like Larry O'Brien, head of the Democratic National Committee, and Edmund Muskie, who was a Democratic presidential candidate.

Amid this tension, Nixon installed a taping system in his presidential offices and in the Cabinet Room. He also had recorders put on several phones. Very few people in the White House knew about the tape recordings, although the Secret Service ran the system. Other presidents had taped conversations, although not as many as Nixon chose to tape. Nixon's system was voice-activated, so that as soon as someone started to talk, the tape began to run. "The existence of the tapes was never meant to be made public," he said later, "at least not during my presidency. I thought that afterward I could consult the tapes in preparing whatever books or memoirs I might write."[1]

In spite of the stress and distrust, there was one bright, family note for the Nixons. On June 12, Tricia Nixon married Edward Cox, a young lawyer, in the White House Rose Garden. But the next morning when Nixon picked up the *New York Times,* he found headlines that wiped out all the happy feelings: VIETNAM ARCHIVE: PENTAGON STUDY TRACES 3 DECADES OF GROWING U.S. INVOLVEMENT.

The *Times* announced that it had in hand a 7,000-page, highly secret study of Vietnam which was done in 1967 at the request of Robert McNamara, who was President Johnson's secretary of defense. The papers were given to the *Times* by Daniel Ellsberg, a former McNamara aide, who had become a fierce opponent of the war.

Throughout his career, Nixon had received the brunt of criticism in the press. " 'They' never let Nixon up," said his speechwriter William Safire. "They applied a double standard to his actions, impugned his motives, derided his squareness and gloried in his defeats."[2]

So Nixon saw these disclosures by the *Times* as a new attempt by the press to hassle and embarrass him even though most of what was in the documents had nothing to do with his administration. In addition, only a small part of the material was confidential or top-secret information that the Communists did not already know. But Nixon was angry. "It is the role of the government, not the *New York Times,* to judge the impact of a top secret document," he said.[3]

He ordered the Justice Department to go to court to try to stop publication of the Pentagon Papers. But on June 30, the Supreme Court ruled against the government six to three, and the *Times* printed the documents in full.

For Nixon, it was a bitter blow. His hated enemy, the press, had beaten him in court. It didn't matter that the Pentagon Papers did not disclose secrets about the Nixon administration. To him, their publication represented a crushing defeat for the power of the U.S. presidency; he believed that the disclosures might interfere with the Vietnam War peace talks. Nixon was also worried that new leaks to the press might endanger his plans to reach out diplomatically to Communist China and to hold arms limitation talks with the Soviets.

He also believed, mistakenly, that other government officials had helped Ellsberg in getting the Pentagon Papers. So instead of accepting the court defeat, he wanted to investigate Ellsberg to learn how he had obtain the papers. Attempts were made to get the FBI to follow Ellsberg's trail, but FBI chief J. Edgar Hoover wasn't interested. Since the FBI would not act, Nixon and his advisers decided they had to take action themselves.

One of Nixon's aides, John Ehrlichman, assigned a young lawyer, Egil "Bud" Krogh, to head up a project to plug the "leaks" of government documents. Three other men, David Young, a lawyer, Howard Hunt, an ex–CIA agent, and G. Gordon Liddy, a former FBI agent, worked for Krogh. The group nicknamed themselves the "Plumbers"—the men who would stop the leaks.

Over Labor Day weekend, some of the Plumbers broke into the office of Ellsberg's psychiatrist in California. They hoped to find information in the files about a conspiracy involving Ellsberg or about Ellsberg's future plans, but they came up with little. "I do not believe I was told about the break-in at the time," Nixon said later, "but it is clear that it was at least in part an outgrowth of my sense of urgency about discrediting what Ellsberg had done and finding out what he might do next."[4]

Whether he was told about the burglary or not is still in question, but clearly Nixon had put heavy pressure on his staff, particularly Krogh, to do something, almost anything, about Ellsberg as soon as possible. If he had been told in advance, Nixon later admitted, he might not have objected to the break-in. His anger against the press had led the law-and-order president to consider breaking the law. It was yet another incident in which the Vietnam War had led an American president to violate the Constitution and the principles for which America stood.

Many Nixon staff members said later that the burglary at the psychiatrist's office represented a serious turning point for the administration. Some of them learned about the break-in shortly afterward, but they did not report it to the police, nor did they even try to ensure that the people involved in the burglary were fired.

Vietnam also took its toll on the nation's economy. Inflation was up due in part to heavy military spending, and the stock market was down. Soon Nixon decided to take strong measures. No longer could foreign governments cash in dollars for gold; the value of the American dollar would be allowed to float. He also imposed a series of freezes on wages and prices, an action he had always said he would not take and that he did not really believe in. The wage-price controls went on until 1974. When they finally ended, inflation soared out of control again.

But during the tense summer of 1971, Nixon pulled off what he called "one of the greatest diplomatic surprises of the century."[5]

Beginning when he was inaugurated, Nixon had made friendly gestures both secretly and openly to China, a nation with whom the United States had broken almost all contact in 1949 when the Communists overthrew the Nationalist Chinese government. Occasionally, the American and Chinese ambassadors met and talked in Warsaw, Poland, but a vast gulf of fear and distrust separated the two nations.

Nixon was fascinated with the idea that he could do what no other modern president had done—bring the two nations together again. He also felt that friendship between China and the United States might speed up the quest for peace in Vietnam.

After his election, Nixon had sent word to China through various foreign officials that he was interested in visiting China. Then in December 1970, Chinese leader Mao Tse-tung told a visitor that he would be happy to have Nixon as his guest.

Soon the State Department lifted restrictions on American travel to China; then Nixon ended a twenty-year-old embargo on trade between the two countries. But one major obstacle still remained: the status of Taiwan, the island nation off the coast of China where the Nationalist Chinese fled after the Communist Revolution. For decades afterward, the United States had insisted that Taiwan's leaders were actually the legal government of China.

In late April 1971, a message was quietly sent to the White House that the Chinese wanted to hold public talks in Beijing with a U.S. envoy or the president to resolve this controversy. Nixon and the Chinese agreed that before Nixon made a visit, Henry Kissinger should go to China first for a preliminary and secret meeting.

Kissinger's visit was planned for the middle of a trip he was making to Asia. While in Pakistan, he supposedly developed a "stomachache" that kept him in bed for a few days. Actually, a Pakistani plane secretly flew him over the mountains to China. There he found the Communist Chinese leaders very eager and interested in a visit by Nixon but still firm on their stand against Taiwan.

On July 15, after Kissinger's return, Nixon triumphantly announced his big news. Richard Nixon, the congressman who in the 1950s had blasted State Department officials and President Truman for "losing" China to the Communists, was going to visit these same Communists. Nixon and Kissinger firmly believed that only Nixon with his strong anti-Communist background could have reached out to Communist China and opened the door. Anyone else, they believed, would have been accused of appeasement and giving in to the Communists.

Although Nixon had been hinting for months that he wanted to visit China someday, the press and public were surprised, and most of the reaction was highly favorable. A few conservatives were upset. One California congressman even accused Nixon of "surrendering to international communism."[6]

Before Nixon left for China, the United Nations General Assembly voted on whether to admit the People's Republic of China, Communist China, as a member, an action which the United States had opposed. But now, the United States withdrew its opposition and said it favored having two Chinas represented in the United Nations. The U.N. General Assembly went further than Nixon and Kissinger had expected and expelled Taiwan while admitting the People's Republic of China.

As the day of Nixon's visit to Beijing drew near, Americans grew more and more excited about this opening in the so-called Bamboo Curtain. U.S. television networks arranged for daily telecasts via satellite of Nixon's trip. Members of Nixon's staff competed fiercely for the chance to be one of the lucky ninety or so aides to go with Nixon and Pat to China.

On February 21, 1972, *Air Force One* pulled to a halt at the Beijing airport on a cold but brilliantly sunny winter day. Wind swept the runway and fluttered red banners. On one long, 20-foot-high (6 m) sign, Chinese characters spelled out the slogan "Long live the great unity of the people of the world." The Stars and Stripes flew next to China's red flag. Americans who watched television as Richard and Pat Nixon stepped through the doorway of the plane knew they were seeing a great moment in history.

Although no cheering throngs greeted the Nixons, Chinese premier Chou En-lai, standing at the foot of the ramp, began clapping his hands, a Chinese gesture of welcome, and Nixon did the same. As Nixon reached the bottom of the stairs, he clasped Chou's hand. Everyone stood at attention as the Red Army band in long coats with fur collars played "The Star-Spangled Banner" and China's national anthem. The Nixons and Chou then climbed into a special black limousine and rode through quiet streets barren of people to a downtown guesthouse where the Nixons were to stay.

The Nixons were guests at special banquets; they visited the Peking Opera, a gymnastics and table tennis exhibition, and the Great Wall of China. They were taken to Hangchow in eastern China, a fairytale city of lakes and gardens.

Nixon had friendly talks with Chou and Chairman Mao Tse-tung about Vietnam, Japan, and Taiwan, although no major agreements were reached. Instead, the two sides wrote a joint statement, the Shanghai Communique, that basically said that they agreed to disagree. The U.S. side supported its eight-point peace plan for Vietnam proposed the month before in Paris; the Chinese endorsed a seven-point plan proposed by the Vietcong. The Communists claimed they were the sole legal government of China and that Taiwan was a province of China. The U.S. recognized this difference of opinion and said that it wanted the Taiwan issue settled peacefully. Both nations opposed any country's seeking to dominate the Asian Pacific region.

It was not an earthshaking statement, but it was a bond between two very different nations, a process of reaching out that had not existed before. Many people believed that this visit to China represented Nixon's greatest accomplishment in office as president.

On the night of the last banquet in China, Nixon raised his glass in a toast and told his hosts, "We have been here a week. This was the week that changed the world."[7]

CHAPTER FIFTEEN

THE RACE FOR
A SECOND TERM

T H E triumph in China breathed new life into Nixon's presidency and boosted his chances for reelection. While he was scoring new points with voters with his visit to China and also with a Soviet summit, the Democrats seemed to stumble in their quest to find an opponent to Nixon.

In addition, Americans were experiencing a new prosperity that made them unlikely to seek a change in leaders. Real earnings were up, and Nixon's policies had begun to take a bite out of inflation, if only temporarily. Nixon had poured money into mass transit, education, and the arts. He was working on reorganizing and streamlining the federal bureaucracy. He had eliminated income taxes for millions of low-income people. He was pushing for elimination of production controls for farmers. He was moving toward reducing regulation in the transportation and banking industries.

With all these factors in his favor, Nixon and his staff grew confident about his prospects of being reelected. But still, the press and dissident groups annoyed and frustrated them. After all, the war was grinding on in Vietnam and as long as young soldiers were dying, Nixon was vulnerable. The feeling remained that somehow the Democrats might pull off an upset victory by using Vietnam to their advantage.

In the past, the Democrats had sometimes pulled "dirty tricks," or practical jokes, to embarrass the Republicans in their campaigns. This time, Nixon's staff decided they wanted their own dirty tricks. Nixon even told Haldeman and other advisers that he wanted the Democratic candidates as annoyed and embarrassed as he had been in the past.

Dwight Chapin, Nixon's appointments secretary, hired a college classmate, Donald Segretti, to pull off some of these tricks. For example, Segretti printed flyers inviting people to a free lunch at one candidate's offices; he ordered 200 pizzas sent to a big fund-raising dinner for another Democrat. These activities could be viewed as silly pranks, but he also sent out letters with false return addresses in which he charged that some candidates were immoral or mentally unstable.

Nixon's staff also kept up the push for campaign intelligence, to find out as much as possible about what the Democrats were planning and to uncover any secrets that the Democrats might be hiding. As part of this effort, G. Gordon Liddy, who had been involved in the break-in at Daniel Ellsberg's psychiatrist's office, was hired as financial counsel, or attorney, for Nixon's Committee to Re-Elect the President. Liddy's job did not involve legal and financial work so much as trying to develop plans to disrupt the Democratic presidential campaign.

In early 1972, Liddy outlined to Nixon staff members what he had in mind. The meeting was held in the office of Attorney General John Mitchell, who would soon resign to head up the Committee to Re-Elect the President. According to John W. Dean III, serving as legal counsel to Nixon, Liddy proposed infiltrating antiwar groups with paid spies. He also suggested kidnapping hostile radical leaders who showed up for the Republican Convention in San Diego and then holding them in Mexico until the convention was over. He talked about using wiretaps to intercept conversations of Democrats.

The proposals were outlandish and expensive, and Dean claimed that he was shocked and upset. At first, Mitchell turned Liddy down. But Mitchell was under pressure from Nixon's chief of staff, Haldeman, to come up with some kind of intelligence plan. So eventually he approved a modified proposal including wiretapping and bugging to be used on the Democrats.

Exactly what Mitchell approved and how much he knew about the details of Liddy's plans are still in question. Mitchell's deputy, Jeb Stuart Magruder, was also in on the decision-making involving Liddy. Some contended that Mitchell was so involved with personal problems involving his wife and a scandal involving a lobbyist that he failed to supervise Magruder and Liddy properly.

In his memoirs, Nixon insisted that he did not know what Liddy and Mitchell were considering, although several other members of his staff did.

Then on June 17, 1972, the bombshell hit. Five men were arrested early that Saturday morning in the headquarters of the Democratic National Committee inside the swanky Watergate hotel-office complex on the banks of the Potomac River in Washington.

The group carried a walkie-talkie, forty rolls of film plus two cameras, bugging devices, lock picks and pen-size tear-gas guns. Clearly, the men intended to electronically bug the offices to pick up conversations about campaign plans. In fact, it was their second secret visit to Watergate. They were actually returning to fix some equipment that had broken.

One of the burglars was James McCord, a retired CIA agent who also worked as security coordinator for the Committee to Re-Elect the President. The other burglars included Cuban-Americans who had been active in anti-Castro activities. The men had been hired by Gordon Liddy and Howard Hunt, another former CIA agent, and they had been paid at least in part for the job from a slush fund of cash campaign contributions from the Committee to Re-Elect the President.

At first, the news of the break-in aroused little attention. Nixon was on vacation in Florida at his Key Biscayne retreat at the time and read about the break-in first in a newspaper. "It sounded preposterous: Cubans in surgical gloves bugging the DNC!" he later wrote. "I dismissed it as some sort of prank."[1]

But soon at the *Washington Post,* two young reporters, Carl Bernstein and Bob Woodward, began investigating the story that would obsess them for years to come. Day after day, they uncovered more and more little bits of information about the burglary, until the story gradually grew into a monster that threatened to devour all that Nixon had accomplished.

But as Nixon returned to the White House at the end of the weekend, Watergate seemed only a little worry compared to Vietnam and the economy and the Soviets. In his diary at the time, Nixon wrote that Haldeman had told him of McCord's link to the Committee to Re-Elect the President. "I told Bob," he wrote, "that I simply hoped that none of our people were involved for two reasons—one, because it was stupid in the way it was handled; and two because I could see no reason whatever for trying to bug the national committee."[2]

But gradually, Nixon learned that several people besides McCord at his election committee and at the White House were involved with the burglary. In spite of this, he claims, he believed at first that John Mitchell was innocent of any wrongdoing.

During these early days after the burglary, Nixon's staff members were in shock, and those who had any involvement or knowledge of the scheme were issuing denials and blaming each other and trying to cover their tracks.

As the revelations in the press continued, the links to the Nixon presidential campaign grew stronger. Two of the burglars had been carrying address books that listed the name of Hunt, a White House consultant working for Charles Colson, special consultant to the president. Hunt, meanwhile, had temporarily disappeared.

The Democrats were outraged. Larry O'Brien, chairman of the Democratic National Committee, told the press that the Watergate incident "raised the ugliest questions about the integrity of the political process that I have encountered in a quarter century of political activity."[3]

Soon the Democrats filed a civil lawsuit against Nixon's campaign committee, and worries increased for Nixon's staff. They feared that the suit would uncover other embarrassing actions by Nixon's presidential campaign committee.

Nixon and his staff hoped that the Watergate burglars would be quickly prosecuted and given light sentences and that the matter would end there. After all, the burglars had no prior criminal records. Nixon's staff did not want law enforcement officials to investigate too vigorously or they might start prosecuting White House employees.

At first, the White House seemed to cooperate with the investigation. Gordon Liddy was fired from the Committee to Re-Elect the President for refusing to answer questions from the FBI, which was investigating the break-in. Liddy had assured Nixon staff members that he would take full responsibility for the break-in and would not talk too much or blame anyone higher up. But the FBI was not satisfied with Liddy's silence, and FBI agents kept uncovering new information.

On June 23, Haldeman told Nixon that unless action were taken, the FBI would soon trace money paid to the burglars to the Committee to Re-Elect the President. At that point, Nixon made a fatal mistake. He agreed with Haldeman that the investigation had to stop. He told Haldeman to see to it that the FBI backed off. The FBI should be told, Nixon agreed, that if the probe continued, it would dig up information about the long-ago Bay of Pigs invasion of Cuba under President John F. Kennedy. In doing so, the FBI would embarrass another government agency, the CIA, Nixon said.

At first the FBI seemed ready to hold off, but later the new director, Patrick Gray, who had recently replaced J. Edgar Hoover, told Nixon that he was angry about the White House interference. Nixon then told Gray to press on with the investigation. "We have to live with this one," Nixon wrote in his diary, "and hope to bring it to a conclusion without too much rubbing off on the presidency before the election."[4]

In looking back on these early days of the Watergate crisis, many say that if Nixon had torn away the blanket of secrecy then and fired everyone who had any blame for the break-in or similar operations, he might have been reelected anyway and survived the crisis with little damage. But Nixon viewed Watergate as a political battle just like the one he faced in the 1950s over his campaign fund. "I saw Watergate as politics pure and simple," he said. "We were going to play it tough. I never doubted that that was exactly how the other side would have played it."[5]

The investigation took its toll on Nixon's campaign director, John Mitchell, and on July 1, 1972, Mitchell resigned his post. Losing Mitchell was painful for Nixon. They had become close friends while working together as lawyers in New York. Things had just gotten out of control for Mitchell, Nixon thought. He felt he had to protect Mitchell from further damage.

In spite of the Watergate mess, Nixon's campaign for reelection steamed ahead. During the Democratic primaries, George McGovern, a senator from South Dakota who strongly opposed the war in Vietnam, had beaten back other candidates. But when the Democrats staged their convention in Miami in July 1972, they were again engulfed in turmoil, not the same kind as in 1968, but equally deadly to their chances of electing a president.

After 1968, the Democrats had reformed their party rules so that many of the mistakes made at the Chicago convention would not happen again. The idea was to take the nomination process out of the hands of the professional politicians and put it in the grasp of the people at the bottom, including women, minorities, and groups with special interests. But as a result, the platform drafted at their convention contained a number of far-reaching, liberal proposals that the American public as a whole found hard to swallow. Some of the more extreme proposals were left out of the platform, but since the debates on policies were often held late at night, most Americans did not see the discussions and votes on television.

McGovern, who had led the reform drive, finally succeeded in getting his delegates seated at the convention. But to do so, he had to battle a coalition of political leaders who opposed him. In the process, he alienated many powerful people whose support he needed in order to win the election.

On the night that a vice president was to be chosen and McGovern was to give his acceptance speech, the convention became chaotic. Several delegates nominated their own choices for vice president, and the speeches and voting droned on and on until long past television prime time. When McGovern finally arrived to give his speech at 2:48 A.M., most Americans had gone to bed. "Even at Chicago in 1968, with all the violence, bloodshed and dissension, the party had pulled itself together well enough to let Hubert Humphrey speak to the nation when the nation was ready to listen," said historian Theodore H. White.[6]

Shortly after the convention, another blow fell. McGovern's staff learned that the man chosen as the candidate's running mate, Senator Thomas Eagleton of Missouri, had previously been hospitalized three times for mental illness and had received electroshock treatments. Knowing that newspaper reporters were hot on the trail of the story, McGovern and Eagleton held a press conference to announce this damaging news.

Hundreds of calls and letters poured in pressuring McGovern to drop Eagleton from the ticket. Major newspapers urged Eagleton to quit. Outwardly, McGovern seemed to stand firmly behind his running mate as they traveled the country to campaign. He announced he was "1,000 percent for Tom Eagleton."[7] But behind the scenes there was turmoil. Campaign fund-raising had halted, and the McGovern staff hesitated to spend money on banners and buttons and posters with the names "McGovern" and "Eagleton" on them.

In the end, Eagleton had to go, and confusion followed as McGovern sought another running mate and was turned down by several other people. Finally, Sargent Shriver, the husband of one of John F. Kennedy's sisters, accepted.

Because of his handling of the Eagleton crisis, McGovern went into the fall campaign with his credibility as a candidate shattered. As Theodore White put it: "Lost was McGovern's reputation as a politician somehow different from the ordinary—a politician who would not, like others, do *anything* to get elected."[8]

This turmoil among the Democrats reassured the Republicans. It appeared that all they had to do was sit back and watch their adversaries tear the Democratic Party to shreds in another election.

About the only difficult political question that Nixon had to consider before the Republican convention met in Miami in 1972 was whether to keep Spiro Agnew as his vice president. Nixon thought about replacing Agnew with John Connally, the secretary of the treasury, but in the end, he kept Agnew.

In comparison with the Democratic convention, the Republican convention was a smoothly running machine, carefully engineered to show off the president at his best. There were beautifully made films: a documentary on Pat Nixon's life, a movie that showed the finest moments of Nixon's career in the White House. There were movie stars and celebrities: Sammy Davis, Jr., on stage hugging Nixon during a youth rally.

To be sure, antiwar demonstrators outside the convention hall were throwing rocks and eggs, but inside, the delegates were shouting: "Four more years!"

Finally, after being nominated for a second term by a vote of 1,347 to 1, Nixon spoke to the nation:

> *I ask you, my fellow Americans, to join our new majority not just in the cause of winning an election but in achieving a hope that mankind has had since the beginning of civilization. Let us build a peace that our children and all the children of the world can enjoy for generations to come.*[9]

As he moved closer to what looked like a landslide win in November, only two problems troubled Nixon—Vietnam and the Watergate scandal. But with the kind of mandate he expected to get from the American people, he felt confident of the future.

CHAPTER SIXTEEN

ON THE THRESHOLD
OF PEACE

A L L the while that Nixon pursued his second race for the White House and dealt with the Watergate scandal, he faced a deepening crisis in Vietnam.

After taking office, he had fulfilled his promise to begin withdrawing American soldiers from Vietnam. Originally, the United States had more than a half million men in the conflict, but by the start of the election year, only 139,000 remained. When he took office, some 300 Americans a week were dying in Vietnam; when he was nominated again at the GOP convention, only three or four were dying there each week.[1]

But still his quest for a solution in Vietnam went nowhere. Then in the spring of 1972, the presidential election year, the Communists showed the world how weak the South Vietnamese army really was. On March 30, 1972, 120,000 North Vietnamese and thousands of Vietcong guerrillas rolled in a tremendous wave across the northern and central provinces of South Vietnam.

Nixon talked strongly to the press about how the South Vietnamese were pushing back the invaders, but privately he was anxious and worried. "It is ironic," he wrote in his diary, "that having come this far, our fate is really in the hands of the South Vietnamese."[2]

Nixon believed that the North Vietnamese were tougher, more willing to make sacrifices to win. He began to doubt the will of the South Vietnamese to fight.

As he had done before, Nixon kept pressuring the Soviets, who hoped to hold a summit meeting with the United States. He felt the Soviets should be able to force the North Vietnamese to negotiate. He grew especially angry when the North Vietnamese canceled a meeting with Kissinger set for April 24. He told Kissinger that he would cancel the summit unless the situation improved in Vietnam.

Meanwhile, Nixon scheduled heavy bombing raids against Hanoi and against the North Vietnamese port of Haiphong, through which the Soviets were pouring supplies into North Vietnam. As a result, U.S. bombers accidentally hit four Soviet merchant ships. The Soviets protested, but only mildly. When Kissinger went to Moscow for a presummit meeting, they told him they simply did not have the influence over North Vietnam that the United States seemed to think they had. There was very little that they could do to stop the war.

Kissinger met again with the North Vietnamese on May 2, but talks broke off quickly. More and more, Nixon believed he had to cancel the summit or take harsh action in Vietnam that would lead the Russians to cancel the meeting. He ordered the mining of the Haiphong harbor and bombing of railroad lines in North Vietnam. On the evening of May 8, he gave a televised speech announcing his plans, which he knew the opponents of the war would denounce. But he also made a new peace proposal to North Vietnam—one that was surprisingly softer than some made by the United States in the past. He asked that all American prisoners of war be returned and that a supervised cease-fire be set up in Indochina. After that, he said, he would completely withdraw all American forces from Vietnam within four months. He did not ask that the Communists pull all their troops out of South Vietnam as he had in the past.

In spite of his concessions, Congress was outraged by the new bombing plans. News commentators and columnists predicted that the summit with the Soviets was doomed. The Soviet news agency denounced the mining plans, but a few days after Nixon's speech, the Russian ambassador called Kissinger to set up plans for Nixon's trip to Moscow. The opinion polls showed that Nixon's popularity was rising again.

The trip was a triumph for Nixon. Both sides signed a treaty agreeing to give up some of their missile defenses. This meant that each country left itself open to possible attack by the other side. "Each side therefore had an ultimate interest in preventing a war that could only be mutually destructive," Nixon said.[3] They also signed an agreement freezing the levels of various kinds of missiles temporarily until a permanent agreement could be signed. Nixon made the agreements although he knew the Pentagon opposed the proposals.

Vietnam was discussed, but the Soviets were very cautious in commenting on the topic until the end of Nixon's visit. At that point, the Soviet Communist Party chief, Leonid Brezhnev, offered to send a representative to North Vietnam to plead for peace.

Despite their military gains, the North Vietnamese were beginning to feel the pressure. Nixon's visit to China had surprised them, and his trip to Moscow troubled them, too. The Hanoi newspaper *Nhan Dan* complained that North Vietnam's two chief allies, China and Russia, were betraying "lofty internationalist duties" by being friendly to the United States.[4]

It was true that George McGovern, a strong antiwar candidate, had won the Democratic nomination for the presidency, but the North Vietnamese knew he had little chance of winning. So Nixon would be president for another four years, and the North Vietnamese knew he was not ready to abandon the South Vietnamese government.

Not only that, but Nixon had offered them a compromise allowing them to keep their troops in South Vietnam even if a peace pact were signed. That meant that they might be able to finish off the South Vietnamese government within a few years once the Americans had left Vietnam.

Negotiations resumed in Paris in late September, and the North Vietnamese had a new peace proposal. Although Kissinger was receptive, it still had several key points that the United States did not want. Another meeting was set for October 8.

Although it did not look as if the war could be settled before the election, Nixon and his advisers felt they were on the brink of a major breakthrough that would ensure his victory in the election. One big problem would be winning the support of South Vietnamese president Thieu for the agreement. Thieu was beginning to feel that the United States was abandoning him. An aide was sent to Saigon to reassure Thieu.

On October 8, Kissinger arrived in France amid crisp autumn weather to begin secret meetings with the North Vietnamese in a white stucco house near Paris that had once belonged to the painter Ferdinand Leger. Sitting at a green baize table in a room hung with abstract paintings, the two negotiating sides handed each other their proposals and then broke for an intermission to consider them.

When they returned to the meeting room, North Vietnam's chief negotiator, Le Duc Tho, announced that he wanted to throw out all the rules about the talks that he had previously insisted on. He proposed a cease-fire, U.S. troop withdrawal, and a swap of prisoners of war. The political problems would be resolved later by an "administration of national concord," a council made up of representatives of the Saigon regime and Communists. The governments of both North and South Vietnam and their armies would remain intact. In a sense, the North Vietnamese had accepted Nixon's May 8 proposal. Not only that, but the North Vietnamese wanted the peace pact signed by October 31, when the cease-fire would begin.

For Kissinger, it was one of the most thrilling moments of his career. "At last, we thought, there would be an end to the bloodletting in Indochina. We stood on the threshold of what we had so long sought, a peace compatible with our honor and our international responsibilities," he said.[5]

Kissinger accepted the terms in principle although insisting on holding further talks on the details. He cabled

Nixon to tell him the good news and sent an urgent message to Thieu to grab as much territory as possible around Saigon.

When Kissinger arrived back in Washington on October 12, he went immediately to Nixon's special hideaway office in the Executive Office Building to give him the full details. The two men were excited about Kissinger's success, and they shared a celebration meal of steak and wine as they discussed the prospects for peace. Their chief concern was whether South Vietnam's Thieu would accept the agreement.

On the one hand, Nixon was anxious for the war to be settled, particularly before the election. But on the other hand, he told Kissinger, he still wanted an honorable peace; he was not ready to scuttle the South Vietnamese. He also did not want to sign a peace pact that would unravel soon or produce only a brief lull in the fighting.

Nixon also feared that if a settlement were reached, conservatives might turn on him and accuse him of giving away too much to achieve peace before the election. But on the other hand, if he waited until after the election, the Communists might change their minds and keep on fighting.

In his dairy at the time, Nixon wrote:

I am inclined to think that the better bargaining time for us would be immediately after the election rather than before. Before the election, the enemy can still figure there is an outside chance their man can win or at least that he could come closer and that we, therefore, would be under pressure to have a settlement.[6]

On October 18, Kissinger flew to Saigon and found South Vietnamese officials extremely upset about the terms of the settlement. Although he carried a message from Nixon urging Thieu to accept, as Kissinger later said, "What was success for us—the withdrawal of American forces—was a nightmare for our allies."[7]

To reassure the South Vietnamese, Nixon began airlifting $2 billion in weapons and supplies to Saigon.

As the days drifted on, the North Vietnamese were surprisingly willing to make minor changes in the agreement, but the South Vietnamese kept stalling. Thieu did not say no to the peace proposal, but he did not say yes either. Then on October 23, Kissinger met with Thieu, who rejected several parts of the proposal. In particular, he was upset with a plan to create a National Council of Reconciliation and Concord, which he said would become a coalition government that would rob the South Vietnamese government of its authority. He also wanted North Vietnam to pull all its troops out of South Vietnam.

Until that time, all negotiations had been in secret. Nixon wanted no publicity until after the election in case talks broke down again. But then the North Vietnamese went public; they announced the terms of the agreement and accused the United States of delaying a settlement.

At a White House press conference attended by hundreds of reporters, Kissinger explained that an agreement was in the works but that many details still had to be worked out. But in his opening remarks, he also said, "We believe peace is at hand."[8]

The press pounced on the phrase, and Kissinger and Nixon were immediately sorry that he had said those words. Clearly, no settlement could be reached before the election, and a new target date had to be set for the signing of terms: November 20.

Kissinger and Nixon had to struggle to keep the peace proposal alive. Nixon began to pressure Thieu and told him that if he continued to object, "The essential base for U.S. support for you and your government will be destroyed."[9]

After the proposal became public, Nixon faced heavy criticism from George McGovern and the press. Some antiwar activists charged that Nixon was duping the voters to aid his election chances. Some claimed that the proposed peace terms could have been achieved several years before, thus sparing thousands of American lives. McGovern told reporters: "It is really not clear to me what fundamental change has taken place in the last few days which enables Mr. Nixon to announce, now, that we have a settlement just before we go to the polls."[10] But for McGovern, it was only a last stab at trying to damage the nearly invincible Nixon in some way.

Although Nixon had done only limited campaigning during the race, in the last week he took a last trip through several states, ending up with a rally in Ontario, California. "This . . . is the last time I will speak to a rally as a candidate in my whole life," he told the crowd.[11]

On Election Day, the Nixons returned to the White House. In contrast with past elections, when he had waited tensely for the returns, this time Nixon felt confident and assured. He sat in the Lincoln Sitting Room and listened to one of his favorite pieces of music, *Victory at Sea,* while writing his victory speech. Pat, Tricia, and Julie occasionally dropped by to see him. David Eisenhower and Ed Cox brought him word about what the television networks were reporting. Soon H. R. Haldeman was phoning in vote counts as well.

Nixon fully expected to win, but he did not expect the sweeping victory he achieved—the second biggest landslide in U.S. history. Only Lyndon Johnson, in defeating Barry Goldwater, had achieved a bigger margin. Nixon had received more than 47 million votes, 60.7 percent of the votes cast, compared to McGovern's slightly more than 29 million, or 37.5 percent.

It was Nixon's greatest election triumph, and he should have been overjoyed. The public had endorsed everything he had done in his first four years in office. Not only that, he had also achieved stunning diplomatic triumphs, including his trip to China and his arms pacts with the Soviet Union. Even peace in Vietnam seemed within his grasp. But curiously enough, he felt haunted by gloom, a sense that all was not well. In his diary he wrote: "The rest of the family seemed to think that they got enough of a thrill out of it. I think the very fact that the victory was so overwhelming made up for any failure on my part to react more enthusiastically than I did."[12]

Others noticed Nixon's attitude as well. He had always been isolated in his job, but now he seemed to withdraw even from his closest advisers, Kissinger said. "His resentments, usually so well controlled, came increasingly to the surface," he said. "It was as if victory was not an occasion for reconciliation but an opportunity to settle the scores of a lifetime."[13]

On election night, Nixon's aides and advisers stayed up late celebrating. The next morning, the senior staff gathered to meet with Nixon, who greeted them with a mechanical smile and polite thanks. He said he had been worried that after his reelection his administration might become a "burned-out volcano, fresh out of ideas and energy." That would not happen, Nixon promised.

He then walked out, leaving his chief of staff, Haldeman, to make a startling announcement: everyone had to turn in a resignation immediately; then Nixon would spend a month deciding whether or not to accept the resignations, determining who would stay or go. The group was shocked. "It was the morning after a triumph and they were being, in effect, fired," Kissinger said.[14]

Nixon contended that he wanted to eliminate waste and end what he called "the Eastern stranglehold on the executive branch and the federal government." But he admitted later he had gone too far. Although most staff members kept their jobs, their attitudes changed. "I did not take into account the chilling effect this action would have on the morale of people who had worked so hard during the election," he later said.[15]

For the next few days, Nixon withdrew into a shell. Said Kissinger:

Isolation had become almost a spiritual necessity to this withdrawn, lonely and tormented man who insisted so on his loneliness and created so much of his own torment. It was hard to avoid the impression that Nixon, who thrived on crisis, also craved disasters.[16]

CHAPTER SEVENTEEN

PEACE IN VIETNAM, UNREST AT THE WHITE HOUSE

N I X O N had feared that the North Vietnamese might back down from the peace proposal after the election, and, indeed, they did. The talks dragged on into December, and Thieu, in South Vietnam, still kept insisting on withdrawal of North Vietnamese troops from his territory.

Kissinger recommended to Nixon that he begin bombing North Vietnam again and break off the talks for a while. So on December 17, American planes began reseeding the mines in Haiphong Harbor, and a day later, B-52s began bombing raids over North Vietnam. Some 40,000 tons of bombs were dropped over a heavily populated area of North Vietnam over the next eleven days.

Nixon did not announce the bombing, although the operation was conducted openly and the press quickly learned about it. Commentators and columnists violently condemned the action, but there was little public outcry. Although the bombs were dropped in urban areas, the number of civilians who died was very small. Journalist Stanley Karnow believed that American pilots were concentrating on military targets rather than homes and civilian buildings.

On December 26, the North Vietnamese asked that talks be resumed, and Nixon subsequently stopped the bombings. The talks began again in early January, and finally Thieu agreed to the settlement. He probably realized that the American Congress, with its Democratic majority, would not continue backing the war in Vietnam anyway. Nixon had also warned Thieu that if he didn't sign the peace agreement, the United States would do so alone. Finally, on midnight January 27, the agreement, very similar to the one first proposed in October, was signed, and a cease-fire began in Vietnam. America was not yet officially out of Vietnam, but the end was in sight. "We have finally achieved peace with honor," Nixon had announced.[1]

Meanwhile, the turmoil over Watergate continued, although in later years Nixon and many staff members contended that dealing with Watergate took up only small amounts of their time in the White House. In January 1973, the Watergate break-in defendants were ready to go to trial. Besides the men actually involved in the burglary, Howard Hunt and Gordon Liddy were also being prosecuted. To Nixon's staff it seemed crucial that the defendants plead guilty or at least not talk extensively during the trial about anyone at the White House who had approved their proposals.

In fact, Howard Hunt had told the four defendants from Miami that the White House would take care of them financially. He also held out the promise that Nixon might pardon them and wipe out any prison sentences they might have to serve.

As a result, four of those involved in the break-in changed their pleas to guilty, thus waiving their right to a jury trial, where more evidence of White House involvement in the break-in might be disclosed. The four told the judge the rather fantastic story that they had joined the scheme only in order to help the cause of freeing Cuba from Communist control. Howard Hunt also pleaded guilty. McCord and Liddy went to trial, but very little information not already known to the press came out in their trials.

Behind the scenes, hundreds of thousands of dollars, more than $200,000 in the first few months after the burglary, were raised by Nixon's personal attorney Herbert Kalmbach and delivered to the defendants. Another $200,000 or so of loose cash at the White House was also paid out. Some White House staff members, H. R. Haldeman, John Ehrlichman, John Dean, and others, knew about the money. They told themselves that the money was being paid for benevolent and humanitarian reasons, not as hush money to keep the defendants quiet. "The request, shortly after the burglars had gone to jail, that Kalmbach be asked to raise funds for their legal fees and family support seemed reasonable enough," Haldeman said. "They were our people, working for the Committee for the Re-Election of the President."[2]

Did Nixon approve of the money-raising? He did know about plans for some sort of Cuban Defense Fund back in June 1972, shortly after the break-in, Haldeman contends. But, says Haldeman, he didn't know all the details of the money demands and fund-raising.

Many senators were growing frustrated because the attorney general, the FBI, and the courts were not digging up the full Watergate story. In early February, Democratic senator Sam Ervin of North Carolina began organizing an investigation by the Senate Select Committee on Presidential Campaign Activities. Although Nixon made a stab at trying to stop the investigation, in the Senate's final vote to launch the probe, Republicans joined Democrats in a unanimous vote.

In fact, prominent Republicans were very worried and had pressured Nixon to take some public action in the Watergate matter. Nixon felt betrayed by his own party. He wrote in his diary at the time:

It is hard to understand how those we have supported so strongly have to make asses of themselves by taking up the cry of the opposition on a matter of this sort when they know very well that there could not possibly be any involvement at the White House level.[3]

Nixon debated with his staff whether he could invoke the principle of executive privilege, the president's right to keep some sensitive matters secret, in order to keep his aides from having to testify. At the same time, Patrick Gray, who had been serving as acting head of the FBI, asked Nixon to make him the permanent director of that agency. Nixon agreed, even though he knew that during confirmation hearings, senators would quiz Gray about his actions during the FBI investigation of Watergate.

During the Gray hearings, senators were horrified to find out that John Dean of Nixon's staff, who would become a key figure in the unraveling of the Watergate cover-up, had sat in when FBI agents interrogated White House staff members. Gray had also passed dozens of FBI reports to Dean. Every move that the FBI had made in the probe had been reported to Dean. How could the FBI carry on an impartial investigation when the people it was investigating knew exactly what the FBI was up to? Eventually, Gray's nomination had to be withdrawn.

At this point, Nixon began pushing Dean to do some sort of investigative report about Watergate that he could use in a report to the nation. Dean resisted because he felt there was little he could say without telling the truth, and the truth was too ugly to disclose in full.

At meeting after meeting with Dean and other members of his staff, Nixon was learning more bad news about Watergate—that several staff members had known about Gordon Liddy's intelligence-gathering plans in advance. He also heard the story of the break-in at the office of Daniel Ellsberg's psychiatrist. He was particularly worried about John Mitchell's involvement in the Watergate burglary and John Ehrlichman's involvement in the Ellsberg burglary. Nixon resisted the idea of coming clean and telling the whole story to the public.

Many of these crucial meetings were being recorded on the taping system that Nixon had set up in his office.

On March 21, 1973, a fateful meeting of Nixon and staff members was held, one that came to be called "the cancer on the presidency" meeting. It was a day Nixon later called "a disastrous turning point in my presidency."[4] On that date, he claimed, he first learned about the Watergate cover-up, although it is widely believed that he knew of the criminal involvement of many staff members before then.

At the meeting, Dean briefed Nixon about who had been

involved with what in the Watergate break-in. Nixon also learned that one of the Watergate defendants, Howard Hunt, was pressing for another $122,000 and threatening to tell all about John Ehrlichman's role in the Ellsberg matter if he didn't get the money. "The blackmail is continuing," Dean said.[5] He told Nixon that he expected the Watergate burglars to demand a million dollars over the next two years.

Meanwhile, Dean had grown worried about his own role in the burglary cover-up. He suggested that the only way out for Nixon might be to set up a new grand jury to investigate Watergate. That grand jury, Dean said, could grant him, Dean, immunity so he could testify fully about the details of the cover-up without the threat of going to jail. Dean told Nixon he was afraid that he, Dean, could be indicted for obstruction of justice. "We have a cancer within, close to the presidency, that is growing," Dean said. "It is growing daily."[6]

Some statements that Nixon made at this meeting seem to indicate that he was willing to make the payoff to Hunt and continue the cover-up. "You could get a million dollars," Nixon told Dean. "You could get it in cash. I know where it could be gotten. It is not easy but it could be done."[7] Nixon also indicated that he wanted to continue paying off Hunt at least temporarily in order to buy time to resolve the situation.

But Nixon also commented that he thought eventually the whole story would have to come out. "Well, the erosion is inevitably going to come here, apart from anything, and all the people saying well the Watergate isn't a major issue. It isn't. But it will be. It's bound to."[8]

At times Nixon and his staff discussed the option of coming clean and telling the whole truth to the public, but the idea never seemed to get very far. In most of their meetings, they seemed intent on gathering facts about the break-in and the culprits. But it was information they wanted to use not for turning over to prosecutors or investigators, but for their own purposes. That is, they wanted information useful for developing a strategy for handling the crisis.

Nixon claims that after the meeting with Dean he felt anxious about what might happen to members of his staff who were involved in the break-in. He contends he still had not grasped the huge size of the cover-up. It was like pieces of a puzzle that he couldn't quite fit together, he says. "Only three weeks later when I finally saw the whole cover-up mosaic in perspective and realized the position the payments to the defendants played in it," he said later, "would I understand what Dean had really been trying to tell me."[9]

He still insisted that Dean write a report on the Watergate crisis to give to Senator Ervin's committee. On March 22, 1973, he told Dean he wanted the report regardless of what it meant. "If it opens up doors, it opens up doors," he said.[10]

The very next day, a new bombshell hit as sentencing began for the Watergate defendants. One of them, James McCord, gave Judge John Sirica a letter which said that the defendants had been pressured to plead guilty and keep silent and that lies had been told during his trial. Sirica freed McCord on bond and gave the other defendants tough sentences.

As the latest news broke, family members watched Nixon become more tense and anxious. Over Easter, he traveled with Pat and Julie to Key Biscayne, Florida, but the change of scenery did not lift the gloom. He rarely spoke to those who were with him. He seldom said a word to Pat about Watergate.

By then, Dean had hired a criminal attorney and had gone to federal prosecutors to give them information about the Watergate case in hopes of avoiding prison.

Pressure continued to build. "We could no longer avoid facing the unpleasant fact that the whole thing was completely out of hand," Nixon said, "and that something had to be done to get the White House out in front."[11]

As John Dean told all, information was leaked to the press that pinned blame on John Ehrlichman and H. R. Haldeman in many of the Watergate dealings. How could these two remain on the White House staff, the public wondered, when they had done what they did?

Attorney General Richard Kleindienst and his assistant Henry Petersen came to Nixon and told him that he had to fire his chief aides. Nixon felt both men were largely innocent of any wrongdoing; by firing them, he would be telling the world that they were guilty. "I can't fire men simply because of the appearance of guilt," he told Petersen. "I have to have proof."[12]

Petersen insisted that they had to leave: Ehrlichman because he had reportedly told Dean that Howard Hunt's files should be destroyed, and Haldeman because he allegedly had known about the bugging plans ahead of time.

For the next two weeks, Nixon wavered back and forth about whether to fire the two men. They were peers whom he trusted and on whom he depended. For Nixon, who had never made friends easily, the two were close companions with whom he shared secrets and times of crisis. They had worked hard for him, and their loss would leave serious gaps in the nation's leadership.

Their lawyers pleaded their case with Nixon. "I was selfish enough about my own survival to want them to leave; but I was not so ruthless as to be able to confront easily the idea of hurting people I cared about so deeply," he said.[13]

Finally on April 29, Nixon met with Ehrlichman and Haldeman at the presidential retreat at Camp David. Both tried to reassure Nixon that they accepted the decision. He was deeply shaken and openly told them that the night before, he had hoped "and almost prayed, that I wouldn't wake up in the morning."[14]

Ehrlichman put his arm around Nixon's shoulders and told him, "Don't talk that way. Don't *think* that way."[15]

After the two men left Camp David, an aide, Ray Price, helped him write his announcement of the resignations. At one point, Nixon asked Price if he (Nixon) too, should resign. Price told him no, he had a job that he was responsible for and furthermore Vice President Agnew could not handle it.

On April 30, Nixon finally made his first address to the American people about Watergate. He announced that Haldeman and Ehrlichman had resigned and Dean had been fired. Attorney General Richard Kleindienst was also leaving. Because he had been a close friend of Mitchell's, Kleindienst felt he had to leave his job.

In the television speech, Nixon gave the impression that he had known nothing about the cover-up until his March 21 meeting with Dean, although he had known many details before then. In his memoirs, Nixon admitted he had been deceptive. Although his speech had talked about how he would bear responsibility for his staff's actions, "that was only an abstraction and people saw through it," he said.[16]

Afterward, Nixon seemed like a bent and broken man to his family. He repeatedly asked others whether he should resign.

The television speech had been meant to quiet the Watergate storm, but the explanations Nixon gave the nation had little impact. It was as if a hurricane had hit Washington. Story after story and rumor after rumor were reported by the press, many of them wild and untrue. There were reports that offices of various senators were bugged; that Nixon campaigners had promoted violence at antiwar demonstrations; that there had been several other burglaries pulled off by White House staff members.

A temporary lull took place in the Watergate story in mid-June when Soviet leader Leonid Brezhnev came to Washington for another summit meeting. But as soon as he returned to Moscow, the storm broke again. This time, John Dean went before the Senate's Watergate committee to testify. His most explosive charge was that for six months, ever since a September 15, 1972, meeting, Nixon had been taking part in the Watergate cover-up.

As Nixon listened to Dean testify, he felt Dean was exaggerating some events and twisting others. Nixon listened to some of the Oval Office tapes of their meetings and double-checked the facts. At first he thought he could present his own account to refute what Dean was saying. But then he realized that what he said did not matter. "It no longer made any difference that not all of Dean's testimony was accurate," Nixon said. "It only mattered if *any* of his testimony was accurate."[17]

But soon an even greater crisis would rip the White House. Nixon's top-secret Oval Office tapes were about to become public.

CHAPTER EIGHTEEN

THE TAPES

O N July 13, 1973, in the basement of the New Senate Office Building, two members of the Ervin committee were grilling Alexander Butterfield, an aide to H. R. Haldeman, about the Watergate situation. During the meeting Butterfield revealed news that would soon stun the nation—in his offices, Nixon had been using a taping system to record conversations.

By then, the Watergate crisis had begun to drain Nixon's physical strength. That same day, he had gone through his appointments while his chest throbbed with pain and his temperature soared to 102 degrees. After finishing his daily schedule, he went to Bethesda Naval Hospital to be treated for viral pneumonia.

Early Monday morning, just as he started to feel better, he learned about Butterfield's disclosure about the tapes. The Ervin committee was about to announce their existence to the world. Soon the committee would demand to listen to them. Nixon was shocked. At the height of the Watergate crisis, he and Haldeman had discussed destroying the recordings but never did so. Should he destroy the tapes now? Should he claim executive privilege, the supposed right of presidents to keep some information confidential, and prevent the tapes from being reviewed publicly?

As word blared out in the papers and on television, he and his staff kept insisting that previous presidents had also taped conversations—but no one seemed to care. All that interested the press and public was Nixon's tapes and how much they revealed about his involvement in Watergate.

Soon Nixon concluded that although the tapes contained many damaging and embarrassing conversations, on the whole they refuted John Dean's charge that Nixon had covered up Watergate for eight months. He also agreed with his new chief of staff, Alexander Haig, that if he destroyed the tapes, everyone would immediately say he was guilty of all that Dean had said.

But he decided to fight to keep the tapes secret even though it made him look as if he were hiding his guilt. He said:

> *I know that most people think that executive privilege was just a cloak that I drew around me to protect myself from the disclosure of my wrongdoing. But the fact that I wanted to protect myself did not alter the fact that I believed deeply and strongly in the principle.*[1]

A key figure in the fight about the tapes was Archibald Cox, whom the new attorney general, Elliott Richardson, had appointed as a special prosecutor in the Watergate case. Richardson had been pressured to pick a Democrat, someone free from any links to the White House. Cox was not only a Democrat, he was a Democrat with close ties to the Kennedy family, and he chose fellow liberal Democrats for his legal staff. Nixon was upset at Richardson's choice, and it seemed likely that he would end up clashing with Cox, who represented all Nixon detested about the so-called Eastern Establishment.

Cox moved to subpoena some key tapes and so did the Ervin committee, although by then the committee hearings had adjourned. Presumably, Cox wanted to use the tapes to prosecute Nixon staff members, but it was possible he could use them against Nixon as well. Nixon decided to fight the subpoenas in court. But although he was still battling, the fight was sapping Nixon's energy and that of his staff. Some of his Cabinet members quit.

As if Watergate were not enough to handle, Nixon learned that summer that Vice President Spiro Agnew was in serious trouble due to his conduct while he was governor of Maryland. Reportedly, Agnew had taken bribes and kickbacks in return for granting state contracts. Agnew kept insisting that he was innocent and that the money involved could be viewed as political contributions. But Attorney General Richardson insisted that the evidence was real and that Agnew was not being railroaded. By the end of September, it was clear that Agnew had to go. On October 10, 1973, he resigned, in return for which he received a sentence of three years' probation and a $10,000 fine in the case pending against him.

There would be more trying moments during the next few weeks. In some cases, Nixon's responses showed him at his finest as he handled a difficult international crisis. At other moments, he seemed petty, mean, and vindictive, and ultimately he took an action that signaled the end of his presidency.

After Agnew resigned, Nixon pondered several choices for men to become vice president. Among the top candidates were Nelson Rockefeller, Ronald Reagan, John Connally, and Gerald Ford. In the end, Nixon chose Ford, who was the minority leader in the House of Representatives. He knew that the Democrats approved of his choice because they viewed Ford as a caretaker in the job, someone who would not try to run for president in 1976.

But simultaneously, while Nixon was handling the Agnew crisis, war broke out in the Middle East. Syria and Egypt attacked Israel in what was called the Yom Kippur War, since it began on the Jewish Day of Atonement. Some historians believe Israel's enemies might never have attacked if not for Watergate, which they believed had sapped Nixon's political power.

At first the Arabs, heavily armed by the Soviets, forced the Israelis to retreat. Israel counterattacked, but a third of its tanks and one-fifth of its planes were destroyed in early fighting. Henry Kissinger demanded that Nixon resupply the

Israelis or the Arabs would destroy them. Nixon ordered the U.S. Air Force to begin shipping arms; in all more than 22,000 tons of supplies went to Israel. Soon the Israelis were sweeping into Egypt.

At first, the Russians seemed ready to step in and help Egypt. The situation seemed ripe for open war in the Middle East between the United States and the Soviet Union. But Kissinger flew to Moscow to confer with the Soviets in order to sidestep the conflict. Eventually, a cease-fire was negotiated; but at the end of October, the Arabs also imposed a full-scale embargo on oil imports to the United States, leading to long lines at the gas pumps.

But always there was Watergate to worry about. "Week by week, month by month," Nixon said, "we were being worn down, trapped, paralyzed."[2]

On October 12, during the Mideast crisis, the U.S. Court of Appeals ruled against Nixon in the tapes case and ordered him to turn over nine of the tapes to the special prosecutor within a week.

Of course, Nixon could appeal to the Supreme Court, but first, he tried for a compromise. He wanted to submit summaries of the tapes to the prosecutor instead of the tapes themselves. He proposed that John Stennis, a Democratic senator whom he respected, audit the tapes and verify that the summaries were accurate. But Cox was unwilling to accept the proposal. Cox told the press he still wanted the tapes.

Nixon was furious. All along, he had objected to having a Kennedy Democrat like Cox as the special prosecutor. Now Cox was defying him openly. A prosecuting attorney was trying to tell the president of the United States what to do. Cox had gone beyond the bounds of what his job should be, Nixon said.

On Friday night, October 19, Nixon announced his compromise proposal to the nation, but the next day he began taking steps to get rid of Cox. "I felt that he was trying to get me personally, and I wanted him out," Nixon said.[3]

Nixon's aide Haig told Richardson to fire Cox. Richardson refused and resigned himself. Next, Richardson's deputy, William Ruckelshaus, resigned rather than fire Cox. Finally, the third-ranking official in the Justice Department, Solicitor General Robert Bork, agreed to tell Cox he was finished. Years later, Robert Bork's role in this matter would hurt him when President Ronald Reagan nominated him to serve on the Supreme Court. (Bork's nomination was rejected.)

The firing of Cox and the resignations outraged reporters, who called it "the Saturday Night Massacre." An hour after the announcement, cars began honking outside the White House and protesters held up signs saying, "Honk for impeachment!"[4]

The hurricane continued to roar through Washington. Although Nixon had expected some protests, he was surprised that even his past supporters were upset and angry. Within ten days, almost 500,000 telegrams poured into the White House and Congress, most of them condemning Nixon's actions. Newspaper editorials demanded his resignation or impeachment.

Nixon was stunned. "For the first time, I recognized the depth of the impact Watergate had been having on America," he said.[5]

Because of the pressure over the firings, Nixon had to accept the appointment of yet another special prosecutor. This time it was Leon Jaworski, a Houston lawyer and prominent Democrat, but Jaworski was someone whom Nixon did not fear as much as Cox.

Soon more shocking news came out about the tapes which Nixon was to give to Watergate judge John Sirica while appealing his case to the Supreme Court. The tape of a key conversation between Nixon and Haldeman on June 20, 1972, had an eighteen-and-a-half-minute gap in it. Nixon's secretary, Rose Mary Woods, told the court she had accidentally erased part of the tape while transcribing it because she was unfamiliar with the tape recorder she was using. The tape gap caused a new uproar. Was it a deliberate attempt to erase key evidence?

Electronics experts examined the tape for a grand jury.

Some concluded that the erasure had been deliberate. Others said it could have been due to a mechanical problem. But in the public's eyes, new evidence had been found that Nixon was trying to cover up his guilt.

Besides the Watergate ordeal, Nixon faced sharp public questions about government-financed improvements made in his own property—his vacation houses in Florida and San Clemente, California. In all, he had spent $10 million in federal money on these properties, much of it for security and communications devices.

There were also questions about a tax break that Nixon had received for donating his prepresidential papers to the federal government. Although the papers themselves were turned over to the National Archives in March 1969, the legal documents about the donation did not meet a deadline set by Congress. To meet the deadline, lawyers backdated the papers. So Nixon had not made a legally proper gift. Because of that and some other real estate deals, Nixon was ordered to pay almost a half million dollars in back taxes and interest.

The Nixons faced a gloomy holiday season that year. The gasoline crisis caused by the Arab oil embargo meant that they did not even want to use *Air Force One* to fly to their San Clemente home for a temporary escape from Washington. Instead they used a commercial airplane so that no one could complain about them wasting some of the nation's precious fuel on a personal trip.

Dreary rain clouds hung over San Clemente, but Nixon stayed there for seventeen days, perhaps dreading what lay ahead. Back in Washington, he would face a tremendous fight. The House Judiciary Committee was conducting an inquiry of Nixon and considering whether it should recommend that the full House impeach Nixon. If impeached, the Senate would try him.

Nixon tried to view the ordeal ahead as he had looked at past political campaigns, although he had lost much support in his own party. He hired a criminal lawyer for himself, James St. Clair. A key group of his staff met regularly to discuss his defense and strategy.

He wrote a note to himself on January 5: "Above all else: Dignity, command, faith, head high, no fear, build a new spirit, drive, act like a President, act like a winner."[6]

But his actions seemed to label him as a loser. When he returned to the White House, he was often moody and aloof. He was restless and unable to sleep at night. Some aides noticed that he was drinking more, sometimes as early as eleven in the morning.

THE TAPES

CHAPTER NINETEEN

THE FAREWELL

T H R O U G H O U T the winter of 1973–74, the Judiciary Committee seemed to be aimlessly shuffling the evidence and sorting out questions about Nixon.

But his former aides and advisers were beginning to face the consequences in court: Egil Krogh, Herbert Kalmbach, Dwight Chapin, for example. On March 1, the federal grand jury also indicted H. R. Haldeman, John Ehrlichman, Charles Colson, John Mitchell, and others for obstruction of justice or for perjury or lying.

The indictments did not surprise Nixon, but he was still shaken. He was sure that it was impossible for his ex–staff members to have fair trials. He also believed he could not get a fair hearing in the House Judiciary Committee even though its chairman, Peter Rodino, had promised to work with "care and decency and thoroughness and honor."[1] For one thing, several Democrats on the committee had announced that they wanted to see Nixon impeached. One congressman hung "Impeach Nixon" bumper stickers on his office walls.

Soon the Judiciary Committee and the special prosecutor were demanding more and more tapes and presidential documents. There was the possibility that if Nixon did not meet the committee's demands, he might be held in contempt of Congress.

A bold action might swing the tide his way, he thought.

He decided to release to the committee and the public verbatim transcripts of the Watergate tapes in a massive 1,300-page document that became known as the Blue Book.

On April 29, he went on television and announced that the transcripts

include all the relevant portions of all the subpoenaed conversations . . . everything that is relevant is included—the rough as well as the smooth, the strategy sessions, the exploration of alternatives, the weighing of human and political costs.[2]

As soon as the transcripts were released, the press rushed into action. Newspapers printed them word for word and analyzed and editorialized about them. Paperback publishers rushed 3 million copies into print.

Democrats and Republicans alike were shocked by the transcripts of the tapes—not so much by the information that they revealed about Watergate as by the vulgar language and thinking often used by Nixon and his staff. Even Hugh Scott, the Republican Senate minority leader, called them "deplorable" and "disgusting."[3]

"I'm embarrassed to have our kids read this and think it's part of the life I'm in," said Robert Strauss, the Democratic National Committee chairman.[4]

Americans like to think of their presidents as having lofty and idealistic goals; they believe that they are superheroes who speak and act in high-minded ways. The tape transcripts showed that this was not the case, and Americans were not ready to forgive Nixon for that.

Life in the White House "is a rough game," Nixon said, "and the men I have known who have made it there reflect the ability to play rough when necessary and come out on top."[5]

In spite of his release of the transcripts, there were still more battles over the tapes. Leon Jaworski had requested sixty-four of them, which Nixon refused to give. A district court ordered Nixon to turn them over, and he decided to appeal. Jaworski bypassed the Court of Appeals, and the case went immediately to the Supreme Court.

More and more, Nixon became isolated from his staff and unable to make decisions. Foreign-policy questions still intrigued him, but he seemed to have lost all interest in the nation's domestic problems. Much of the running of the country was left in the hands of his chief of staff, Alexander Haig. During his last few weeks in office, he was rarely in Washington. He spent much of his time at San Clemente, Key Biscayne, or Camp David, and he also made two final trips abroad.

After Kissinger had arranged a peace agreement in the Middle East, Nixon decided to make several personal visits to Egypt, Syria, Saudi Arabia, Jordan, and Israel to help cement the pact during the early summer of 1974. Cheering crowds greeted him everywhere, and when he returned, the House Judiciary Committee's impeachment effort seemed to have stalled. He returned only briefly and then went off for another summit in Moscow in late June and early July.

During these trips, Nixon developed new physical problems. This time, phlebitis, a blood clot, in his left leg caused painful swelling that made walking difficult. There was also the threat that a piece of the clot might break off and travel elsewhere in his body where it could kill him. He refused to call off his travels or ease up on his schedule and did not publicize the illness.

When he returned to Washington, the clock was ticking, and finally the Judiciary Committee scheduled its hearings on impeachment for July 24. Nixon had hoped that he would have the support of a group of his backers on the committee—the Republicans and conservative Democrats. But one by one, his supporters dropped away from him.

The morning of July 24, there was an even greater blow when the Supreme Court ruled against Nixon on the question of the tapes. "The generalized assertion of [executive] privilege must yield to the demonstrated specific need for the evidence in a pending criminal trial," said Chief Justice Warren Burger, one of Nixon's appointees to the Court.[6]

Nixon had to turn over sixty-four tapes immediately. He was particularly worried about the tape for June 23, 1972, in which he and Haldeman had discussed trying to get the CIA to stop the FBI from investigating the Watergate burglary. Nixon's senior advisors, such as Al Haig, agreed that this amounted to "a smoking gun," real proof that Nixon had been guilty of obstruction of justice. But Nixon continued to make excuses and tried to find a way out. He insisted that he had done nothing wrong, even after listening to the tapes again himself.

Even without hearing this crucial tape, the Judiciary Committee voted over the next few days to recommend that the full House impeach the president based on three articles or violations of law: obstruction of justice, abuse of power, and defiance of committee subpoenas. Nixon was at San Clemente, getting dressed after a swim, when an aide called to tell him about the committee's first vote. "That was how I learned that I was the first president in 106 years to be recommended for impeachment: standing in the beach trailer, barefoot, wearing old trousers, a Banlon shirt and a blue windbreaker emblazoned with the Presidential Seal," he said.[7]

In his mind, Nixon faced the possibility that he might have to resign. He began to weigh the question of how he would meet expenses if he left office, particularly with his new tax problems. Could he sell off some of his property in Florida? Could he sell his memoirs?

When Nixon returned to Washington, he found the city engulfed in gossip and rumors about the impeachment vote. He did not want to quit; he did not want to set a new and dangerous precedent for future presidents. But he knew that his power had been severely crippled, that his ability to run the country would be shattered once the impeachment proceedings began.

He also knew: "If I decided to stay and fight, the outcome of the fight was all but settled: I would be defeated and dishonored, the first President in history to be impeached and convicted on criminal charges."[8]

On August 1, 1974, Nixon first told Alexander Haig that he planned to resign. But then he wavered back and forth for several days as he sought the advice of people he trusted. On August 2, one of his chief supporters in the House, Representative Charles Wiggins, had been called to the White House to read a transcript of the "smoking gun" tape. After reading the document, Wiggins was stunned. He told Haig that impeachment was a certainty. There was no escape for Richard Nixon.

Nixon speechwriters Ray Price and Patrick Buchanan also read the transcripts, and they agreed that Nixon had to resign.

Next Nixon met with his family—Pat, Julie, Tricia, David Eisenhower, and Ed Cox—to explain the inevitable. The family gathered in the Lincoln Sitting Room, where Nixon told them about the tape and what it said and his plans to resign. Tricia, Julie, and Ed were opposed to his resigning; David was undecided. Pat told Nixon she was ready to fight to the finish. Later Tricia wrote: "Upstairs Mama, Ed, and I went to the third floor to say good night to Julie and David. We all broke down together and put our arms around each other in circular, huddle-style fashion. Saying nothing."[9]

For several hours, Nixon brooded in lonely silence. Then he called his staff and told them he had changed his mind again. Stop work on his resignation speech, he told them. He was not ready to quit yet. Instead, he would go on television Monday night, August 5, to release the tapes and see what the public had to say about them.

Haig, Price, and Buchanan were shocked that Nixon still thought he had a chance to save his job. But they also felt they could not force him into making a decision. They could not quit their jobs either, they decided, because that would leave Nixon solely dependent on his family for advice.

By the next day, Nixon had a new plan. He had to release the tapes, but he would not speak on television. In a written statement issued Monday night, he admitted to the nation that he had held back evidence from the House Judiciary Committee and kept it a secret from his lawyers. Soon, even some of Nixon's closest supporters were demanding his resignation.

The next morning, Nixon met with his Cabinet and explained his stand. He told the Cabinet members he had considered resigning but had decided not to for fear of setting a dangerous precedent for future presidents. He urged the Cabinet members to concentrate on their jobs over the next few weeks. But after the meeting, he told Henry Kissinger privately that he was still going to leave soon.

Alone, feeling deserted by nearly everyone who had ever supported him, Nixon wrote notes for his resignation speech. He called Haig and his press secretary Ron Ziegler to his office and told them, "Things are moving very fast now, so I think it should be sooner than later. I have decided on Thursday night [for his resignation]. I will do it with no rancor and no loss of dignity."

His parting words to them: "Well I screwed it up good, real good, didn't I?"[10]

Still, there were voices all around Nixon urging him to stay and fight. His daughters and their husbands urged him to delay a decision, as did H. R. Haldeman, who phoned Nixon from California.

But finally, the Nixon family met in the solarium on Wednesday night. The decision had been made, the end was near. They shed tears and held hands as the official presidential photographer took final photos. Nixon had felt that someday they would want to talk about that night together and they would want pictures to remember it by. At the end, Julie burst into tears and embraced her father. They ate dinner together after that and tried to talk, but mostly they were silent.

The next day, Nixon worked on his resignation speech and talked to his successor, Vice President Gerald Ford.

At two minutes before nine that evening, Nixon, in a dark blue suit with an American-flag pin in his lapel, passed through the hallways already stacked with packing boxes and walked into the Oval Office. A few moments later, he sat behind his desk and solemnly told the nation his news. He no longer had enough support in Congress, he said. The next day at noon, he would resign the presidency. "By taking this action, I hope that I will have hastened the start of that process of healing which is so desperately needed in America," he said.[11]

Henry Kissinger walked with Nixon back to the White House family quarters and tried to comfort him. There Nixon's family members met and embraced him. After that, Nixon made final phone calls to apologize to people whom he felt he might have let down. He told one former aide that he wasn't afraid to go to jail if he had to; he might get some writing done there. Leon Jaworski had already informed him that he was an unindicted co-conspirator in several of the Watergate cases. The Watergate defendants had asked him to pardon them before he left office, but Nixon decided he could not do that.

Nixon began the next morning, Friday, August 9, 1974, the 2,027th day of his presidency, by sketching out a few brief remarks to make to his staff members in a good-bye speech. Then he met his family downstairs in the East Room. Pat and Tricia were upset to find out the television cameras would be rolling once again to record their final agony. "That's the way it has to be," Nixon said. "We owe it to our supporters. We owe it to the people."[12]

Loud applause greeted Nixon as he entered the room to the music of "Hail to the Chief," and tears filled many eyes. The White House staff was still loyal, even if the rest of the world had turned its back on the president. Nixon stood at the podium and talked about the long road he had followed from the lemon groves of Yorba Linda to the White House. When things go wrong in life, we think that all is ended, Nixon told the crowd. Not true, he said, it is only a beginning.

"The greatness comes not when things go always good for you, but the greatness comes and you are really tested when you take some knocks, some disappointments, when sadness comes."[13]

Finally it was over and while the staff clapped wildly, the

Nixons filed out down a red carpet to the presidential helicopter that was to take them to Andrews Air Force Base. There they would board *Air Force One* for the flight to San Clemente, California. In front of the helicopter, Jerry Ford shook Nixon's hand in farewell.

As the chopper lifted into the sky, Nixon looked down as the scene below disappeared—the jewel-like green lawn, the imposing White House and memorials of Washington, D.C.

"There was no talk," Nixon said. "There were no tears left. I heard Pat saying to no one in particular, 'It's so sad. It's so sad.' "[14]

That afternoon, Gerald Ford took the oath of office and told the nation, "Our long national nightmare is over." He asked for prayers for Richard Nixon and his family.

CHAPTER TWENTY

NIXON AND HISTORY

A F T E R Nixon left the White House for San Clemente, his troubles were far from over. Congress could no longer impeach him, but he still faced the prospect of being indicted for the Watergate cover-up. Dozens of civil lawsuits were also being filed against him. Nixon was also fighting in the courts to recover his presidential papers from the new administration. His legal fees were mounting into the hundreds of thousands of dollars. The Nixons believed that the outside world was obsessed with the idea of punishing them.

But on September 8, 1974, the president, Gerald Ford, announced a pardon for all crimes or offenses Nixon might have committed from January 20, 1969, through August 9, 1974, the date of his resignation. Some questioned whether Nixon could be pardoned for crimes that he had never been charged with, but no prosecutor seemed ready to press the issue.

Although Nixon's legal troubles were far from over, Ford's pardon at least eliminated the chance that Richard Nixon might go to jail as did more than a dozen of his former staff, including John Mitchell, H. R. Haldeman, John Ehrlichman, and John Dean.

Congress, the press, and many among the American public were outraged at the news of the pardon. It seemed that Nixon would never be punished. The pardon ensured that he would continue to receive his federal pensions and all the benefits given to former presidents.

But for Nixon, the pardon was also psychological punishment. It represented an admission that he was guilty of something, although no one could say exactly what his offenses were. The very day that the pardon was announced, Nixon suffered a severe attack of pain due to the phlebitis in his left leg. Doctors found that a blood clot had broken off in his leg and traveled to one of his lungs. He was hospitalized for five days.

As soon as he returned home, the upheaval in Washington reached out to California again. Judge Sirica threatened to call Nixon to testify in the Haldeman–Ehrlichman–Mitchell case even though Nixon's doctors contended he was not well enough to do so.

While that issue was being debated, Nixon's illness flared up again. He went back to the hospital for an operation to correct problems due to another blood clot. After surgery, Nixon suffered internal bleeding and went into severe shock. Although some believed that his illness might have been exaggerated to keep him out of court, his health was severely shattered, and doctors were surprised that he didn't die. Pat and his daughters hovered at his bedside for two days. By the time he had recovered to the point where he could have testified in Washington, the Watergate trials had ended.

Still Nixon had severe financial problems, made worse by the tax penalties he had to pay. Many of the servants and office staff who had helped run his San Clemente estate had to be let go. The grounds and buildings fell into disrepair. Nixon's one hope was that he could sell his memoirs and possibly do some television interviews in order to pay his bills.

Eventually, he sold the television rights for interviews to British producer–TV personality David Frost for $600,000. There was an outcry over the steep price. The public was not ready for Nixon to make any money off his alleged crimes. The plan was for Frost to interview Nixon for twenty-six hours, footage which was to be trimmed down to six and a half hours of TV viewing.

In spite of his troubles, Nixon began to bounce back, although slowly at first. He would not give up or give in—just as he had promised on the day he left the White House. His physical recovery and his fight to get back in the black financially seemed partly due to courage and partly due to the need to show the world he wasn't finished yet. One morning as he ate breakfast, Pat said to him, "Dick, I don't know how you keep going." His answer: "I just get up in the morning to confound my enemies."[1]

Yet at first, the Nixons remained hidden away at San Clemente, rarely going out even to visit friends. They were stunned at the news that came to them from the outside world: about the prison sentences for his ex–staff members, and about the fall of South Vietnam to the Communists.

But gradually, the Nixons began to take tiny steps toward contact with the outside world. In 1976, Nixon and his wife took an unofficial eight-day visit to the People's Republic of China at the invitation of Mao Tse-tung.

Then, later in the year, there was another heavy blow. The Nixons were stunned by the publication of *The Final Days,* the second book that the reporting team of Carl Bernstein and Bob Woodward had written about the last days of the Nixon White House. The authors claimed that the Nixons had an unhappy marriage and that Mrs. Nixon had a drinking problem.

Against her husband's wishes, Mrs. Nixon borrowed a copy of the book from a secretary in his office and read part of it. Besides the stress of the book, she had had other unhappy news that day: word that Nixon was about to be disbarred as a lawyer by the New York State Bar. It was unlikely he would ever try to practice law again, but the disbarment was a heavy blow. That afternoon, Pat Nixon had a stroke that partly paralyzed her left side.

In many ways, the Nixons' last years in the White House had been disturbing to their marriage. The glitter of Washington power and politics had consumed Nixon and almost destroyed his family life. But after leaving Washington, the Nixons' troubles had brought them closer together than they had been in some time. Nixon was devastated by Pat's illness and clung closely to her bedside until she began to recover.

In 1977, Nixon finally did the long-promised interviews with David Frost. In them he said he had made mistakes but he had not committed the crime of obstruction of justice that so many had accused him of. He had not thought of what he was doing as a cover-up, he insisted. But he also told Frost:

> *I let down my friends. I let down the country. I let down our system of government and the dreams of all those young people that ought to get into government. . . . I let the American people down. And I have to carry that burden with me for the rest of my life.*[2]

An estimated 50 million Americans tuned in to watch Frost interview Nixon. Afterward, the Gallup Poll found that 44 percent of those who watched came away feeling more sympathetic toward him; but 72 percent of those who watched still believed he was guilty of obstructing justice.

Nixon went on to complete his memoirs, *RN: The Memoirs of Richard Nixon,* for which the publisher had paid him a $2.5 million advance. Although reviews for the book were not good, it quickly went to the top of the best-seller lists and stayed there for months. It was the first of several books that Nixon would write after leaving the White House, books that became his economic salvation but also expressed his political views. Among them were *The Real War; Leaders; Real Peace; No More Vietnams;* and *1999.*

In general, Nixon's books repeated some of the same stands he had taken in the past: that America must remain a strong world power and maintain its diplomatic and military ties to other nations. Just because America had floundered in Vietnam, he said, it did not mean that the country should not try to maintain freedom in developing Third World nations. Although he welcomed the peaceful overtures of the Soviet Union in the 1980s and 1990s, Nixon said he believed that the United States must still remain a strong military power and build strong ties with its friends around the world.

These books kept Richard Nixon in touch with the nation; his views were discussed and debated in spite of the fact that he was out of office and out of power in Washington.

Eventually, the Nixons began making more personal appearances outside the world of San Clemente. Then in 1980, they decided to move to New York City to live closer to their daughters and their new grandchildren. After a year in a townhouse in Manhattan, they bought a home in Saddle River, New Jersey.

Increasingly, Nixon was making visits to foreign countries to see the leaders he had visited as president. He was asked by President Ronald Reagan to serve as part of the official United States delegation to Egypt in 1981 for the funeral of the assassinated Egyptian leader Anwar Sadat.

The wounds left by the Nixon presidency had healed so well that in 1982 the chief 200 members of the Nixon administration actually held a reunion in Washington. Nixon attended, of course, but also there in tuxedoes were such figures as Henry Kissinger, John Mitchell, Gordon Strachan, Dwight Chapin, Charles Colson, and Egil Krogh. Nixon read to the crowd a part of the speech he had given the morning of his resignation. By the time he had finished, many in the room were crying. Nixon went to the piano then and played "God Bless America" and then "Happy Birthday" for someone in the audience with a birthday and then "Let Me Call You Sweetheart."

In Yorba Linda, California, the farmhouse where Nixon was born has since been restored as a museum. Across the street a $25 million presidential archive and library have opened. The complex is far more modest than the Ronald Reagan library in Ventura County, but still it symbolizes growing acceptance of Nixon and his role in the history of his country.

Many years must pass before historians and politicians can fully assess the impact of Nixon's time in office. But gradually, the American public has been more willing to look past Watergate and focus on Nixon's accomplishments in politics and domestic and foreign policy.

Some already regard Nixon as the most influential president of the second half of this century. After all, Richard Nixon was the one who firmly wrested control of the presidency from the Democrats. He forged a new and powerful coalition for the Republicans, making use of the newly powerful and West and Sunbelt states. His victory made possible the presidencies of Ronald Reagan and George Bush, many political experts contend.

Although a Republican, presumably opposed to large federal-spending proposals, Nixon developed new concepts (like revenue sharing) designed to make more effective use of the vast tax money in the hands of Washington.

And few Americans who watched it can ever forget the sight of Nixon emerging from *Air Force One* during his visit to China. His attempts to reach out and find new common ground with the Soviet Union and China seem to foreshadow the policies of glasnost and Mikhail Gorbachev.

Nixon summed it up himself in 1988 in a conversation with newsman John Chancellor. When Chancellor asked how Nixon thought he would be remembered, the former president replied, "History will treat me fairly."[3]

NOTES

Chapter One

1.   Richard M. Nixon, *RN: The Memoirs of Richard Nixon* (New York: Grosset & Dunlap, 1978), 3.
2.   Ibid., 2.
3.   David Abrahamsen, *Nixon vs. Nixon* (New York: Farrar, Strauss & Giroux, 1977), 18.
4.   Jessamyn West, *Hide and Seek: A Continuing Journey* (New York: Harcourt Brace Javanovich, 1973), 238–39.
5.   Fawn M. Brodie, *Richard Nixon: The Shaping of His Character* (New York: Norton, 1981), 40.
6.   Nixon, *RN,* 6.
7.   Mary Skidmore, in *The Young Nixon: An Oral Inquiry,* ed. Renee K. Schulte (Fullerton: California State University, 1978), 78.
8.   Jane Milhous Beeson, in *The Young Nixon,* 56.
9.   Ibid., 70.
10.   Nixon, *RN,* 10.
11.   Bela Kornitzer, *The Real Nixon: An Intimate Biography* (Chicago: Rand McNally, 1960), 47–49.
12.   James Grieves, in *The Young Nixon,* 100.
13.   Mary Skidmore, in *The Young Nixon,* 82.
14.   James Grieves, in *The Young Nixon,* 104.
15.   Nixon, *RN,* 14.
16.   Brodie, *Richard Nixon,* 80.
17.   Nixon, *RN,* 115.

Chapter Two

1.   Richard M. Nixon, *RN: The Memoirs of Richard Nixon* (New York: Grosset & Dunlap, 1978), 15.
2.   Paul Smith, in *The Young Nixon: An Oral Inquiry,* ed. Renee K. Schulte (Fullerton: California State University, 1978), 142.

3. Nixon, *RN,* 16.

4. Ibid., 17.

5. Fawn M. Brodie, *Richard Nixon: The Shaping of His Character* (New York: Norton, 1981), 114.

6. Earl Mazo, *Richard Nixon: A Political and Personal Portrait* (New York: Harper & Brothers, 1959), 24.

7. Paul Smith, in *The Young Nixon,* 143.

8. Nixon, *RN,* 12.

9. Ibid., 19.

10. Charles Kendle, in *The Young Nixon,* 187.

11. Nixon, *RN,* 20.

12. Brodie, *Richard Nixon,* 124.

13. Merton Wray, in *The Young Nixon,* 210.

14. Paul Smith, in *The Young Nixon,* 142.

15. Stephen E. Ambrose, *Nixon: The Education of a Politician, 1913–1962* (New York: Simon and Schuster, 1987), 65.

16. Ralph De Toledano, *One Man Alone: Richard Nixon* (New York: Funk & Wagnalls, 1969), 26.

17. Henry D. Spalding, *The Nixon Nobody Knows* (Middle Village, N.Y.: Jonathan David, 1972).

18. Nixon, *RN,* 20.

19. Brodie, *Richard Nixon,* 125.

20. Ibid., 131.

21. Ibid., 130.

22. Nixon, *RN,* 22.

Chapter Three

1. Fawn M. Brodie, *Richard Nixon: The Shaping of His Character* (Norton, 1981), 134.

2. Richard M. Nixon, *RN: The Memoirs of Richard Nixon* (New York: Grosset & Dunlap, 1978), 22.

3. Ibid., 23.

4. Ibid.

5. Brodie, *Richard Nixon,* 151.

6. Lester Davids, *The Lonely Lady of San Clemente* (New York: Thomas Y. Crowell, 1978), 46–47.

7. Julie Nixon Eisenhower, *Pat Nixon, the Untold Story* (New York: Simon and Schuster, 1986), 58.

8. Ibid., 68.

9. Ralph De Toledano, *One Man Alone: Richard Nixon* (New York: Funk & Wagnalls, 1969), 37.

10. Nixon, *RN, The Memoirs of Richard Nixon,* 27.

11. Ambrose, *Nixon,* 108.

12. Nixon, *RN,* 29.

13. Henry D. Spalding, *The Nixon Nobody Knows,* (Middle Village, N.Y.: Jonathan David, 1972), 141.

14. Ibid., 137.

15. Nixon, *RN,* 35.

16. Jerry Voorhis, *The Strange Case of Richard Nixon* (New York: Popular Library, 1973), 14.
17. Nixon, *RN,* 39.
18. Ibid., 40.
19. Ibid., 41.
20. Ibid., 42.

Chapter Four

1. Richard M. Nixon, *RN: The Memoirs of Richard Nixon* (New York: Grosset & Dunlap, 1978), 43.
2. Ibid., 49.
3. Richard Nixon, *Six Crises* (New York: Doubleday, 1962), 2.
4. Ibid., 8.
5. Nixon, *RN,* 57.
6. Ibid., 62.
7. Nixon, *Six Crises,* 41.
8. Nixon, *RN,* 68.
9. Ibid., 71.

Chapter Five

1. Richard M. Nixon, *RN: The Memoirs of Richard Nixon* (New York: Grosset & Dunlap, 1978), 76–77.
2. Ibid., 78.
3. Ibid., 83.
4. Ibid., 84.
5. Julie Nixon Eisenhower, *Pat Nixon, the Untold Story* (New York: Simon and Schuster, 1986), 114.
6. Nixon, *RN,* 86.
7. Ibid., 89.

Chapter Six

1. Richard M. Nixon, *RN: The Memoirs of Richard Nixon* (New York: Grosset & Dunlap, 1978), 92.
2. Ibid., 93.
3. Richard Nixon, *Six Crises* (New York: Doubleday, 1962), 83.
4. Ibid., 85.
5. Ibid., 87.
6. Nixon, *RN,* 98.
7. Ibid., 101.
8. Ibid., 102.
9. Ibid., 103.
10. Nixon, *Six Crises,* 113.
11. Ibid., 114.
12. Videotape of Richard Nixon's Checkers speech, on file at Indian Valley Colleges library, Novato, California.
13. Ibid.

NOTES

177

14. Nixon, *Six Crises,* 119.
15. Nixon, *RN,* 105.
16. Ibid., 106.
17. Ibid., 108.

Chapter Seven

1. Henry D. Spalding, *The Nixon Nobody Knows* (Middle Village, N.Y.: Jonathan David, 1972), 446.
2. Richard M. Nixon, *RN: The Memoirs of Richard Nixon* (New York: Grosset & Dunlap, 1978), 131.
3. Ibid., 123.
4. Ibid., 125–26.
5. Ibid., 155.
6. Ibid., 149.
7. Richard Nixon, *Six Crises* (New York: Doubleday, 1962), 132.
8. Ibid., 150.
9. Ibid., 160.
10. Ralph De Toledano, *One Man Alone: Richard Nixon* (New York: Funk & Wagnalls, 1969), 203.
11. Nixon, *RN,* 172.
12. Ibid., 178.
13. Nixon, *Six Crises,* 199.
14. Ibid., 202.
15. Ibid., 204.
16. Ibid., 218–19.
17. Ibid., 254–55.
18. Ibid., 257.

Chapter Eight

1. Author's interview with William Bagley.
2. Richard Nixon, *Six Crises* (New York: Doubleday, 1962), 305.
3. Ibid., 459.
4. Fawn M. Brodie, *Richard Nixon: The Shaping of His Character* (Norton, 1981), 419.
5. Nixon, *Six Crises,* 307.
6. Theodore H. White, *The Making of the President 1960* (New York: Pocket Books, 1965, reprint of 1961 Atheneum edition), 344.
7. Nixon, *Six Crises,* 340.
8. Ibid., 356.
9. White, *The Making of the President 1960,* 387.
10. Richard M. Nixon, *RN: The Memoirs of Richard Nixon* (New York: Grosset & Dunlap, 1978), 222.
11. Nixon, *Six Crises,* 372.
12. Julie Nixon Eisenhower, *Pat Nixon, the Untold Story* (New York: Simon and Schuster, 1986), 196.
13. Nixon, *RN,* 223.

NOTES

14. Ibid., 223.
15. Nixon, *Six Crises,* 398.
16. Ibid., 422.
17. Nixon, *RN,* 225.
18. Ibid., 228.

Chapter Nine

1. Richard M. Nixon, *RN: The Memoirs of Richard Nixon* (New York: Grosset & Dunlap, 1978), 232.
2. Ibid., 234.
3. Ibid., 239.
4. Ibid., 237.
5. Julie Nixon Eisenhower, *Pat Nixon, the Untold Story* (New York: Simon and Schuster, 1986), 206.
6. Nixon, *RN,* 240.
7. Author's interview with William Bagley.
8. Nixon, *RN,* 244.
9. Author's interview with William Bagley.
10. Julie Eisenhower, *Pat Nixon,* 213.
11. Nixon, *RN,* 245.
12. Julie Eisenhower, *Pat Nixon,* 213–14.
13. Ibid., 214.

Chapter Ten

1. Richard M. Nixon, *RN: The Memoirs of Richard Nixon* (New York: Grosset & Dunlap, 1978), 252.
2. Ralph De Toledano, *One Man Alone: Richard Nixon* (New York: Funk & Wagnalls, 1969), 328.
3. Nixon, *RN,* 260.
4. Ibid., 265.
5. Ibid., 269.
6. De Toledano, *One Man Alone,* 331.
7. William Safire, *Before the Fall: An Inside View of the Pre-Watergate White House* (New York: Belmont Tower Books, 1975, reprint of Doubleday edition, 1975), 37.
8. Ibid., 38.
9. Nixon, *RN,* 276.
10. Ibid., 291.
11. Ibid., 294.

Chapter Eleven

1. William Safire, *Before the Fall: An Inside View of the Pre-Watergate White House* (New York: Belmont Tower Books, 1975, reprint of Doubleday edition, 1975), 98–99.
2. Theodore H. White, *The Making of the President 1968* (New York: Atheneum, 1969), 67–68.

NOTES

179

3. Richard M. Nixon, *RN: The Memoirs of Richard Nixon* (New York: Grosset & Dunlap, 1978), 298.

4. White, *The Making of the President 1968,* 162.

5. Ibid., 165.

6. Nixon, *RN,* 305.

7. White, *The Making of the President 1968,* 290.

8. Nixon, *RN,* 313.

9. Safire, *Before the Fall,* 54.

10. White, *The Making of the President 1968,* 297.

Chapter Twelve

1. Theodore H. White, *The Making of the President 1968* (New York: Atheneum, 1969), 382.

2. Ibid., 424.

3. Ibid., 418.

4. Joe McGinniss, *The Selling of the President 1968* (New York: Pocket Books, 1970, reprint of Trident Press edition, 1969), 27.

5. White, *The Making of the President 1968,* 433.

6. Ibid., 445.

7. Richard M. Nixon, *RN: The Memoirs of Richard Nixon* (New York: Grosset & Dunlap, 1978), 335.

8. Ibid., 360.

Chapter Thirteen

1. Richard M. Nixon, *RN: The Memoirs of Richard Nixon* (New York: Grosset & Dunlap, 1978), 366.

2. Ibid., 389.

3. Ibid., 409.

4. Ibid., 413.

5. Ibid., 449.

6. Ibid., 450.

7. Ibid., 452.

8. Stanley Karnow, *Vietnam: A History* (New York: Penguin Books, 1984, reprint of Viking Press edition, 1983), 611.

9. Nixon, *RN,* 454.

10. Ibid., 457.

11. Ibid.

12. Ibid., 464.

13. William Safire, *Before the Fall: An Inside View of the Pre-Watergate White House* (New York: Belmont Tower Books, 1975, reprint of Doubleday edition, 1975), 211.

14. Nixon, *RN,* 493.

15. Ibid., 496.

Chapter Fourteen

1. Richard M. Nixon, *RN: The Memoirs of Richard Nixon* (New York: Grosset & Dunlap, 1978), 501.

2. William Safire, *Before the Fall: An Inside View of the Pre-Watergate White House* (New York: Belmont Tower Books, 1975, reprint of Doubleday edition, 1975), 344.

3. Nixon, *RN,* 509.
4. Ibid., 514.
5. Ibid., 544.
6. Ibid., 554.
7. Ibid., 580.

Chapter Fifteen

1. Richard M. Nixon, *RN: The Memoirs of Richard Nixon* (New York: Grosset & Dunlap, 1978), 626.
2. Ibid., 627.
3. Ibid., 628.
4. Ibid., 651.
5. Ibid., 646.
6. Theodore H. White, *The Making of the President 1972* (New York: Bantam, 1973, reprint of Atheneum edition, 1973), 244.
7. Ibid., 269.
8. Ibid., 275.
9. Ibid., 325.

Chapter Sixteen

1. Theodore H. White, *The Making of the President 1972* (New York: Bantam, 1973, reprint of Atheneum edition, 1973), 299.
2. Richard M. Nixon, *RN: The Memoirs of Richard Nixon* (New York: Grosset & Dunlap, 1978), 588.
3. Ibid., 618.
4. Stanley Karnow, *Vietnam: A History* (New York: Penguin Books, 1984, reprint of 1983 Viking Press edition), 646.
5. Henry Kissinger, *The White House Years* (Boston: Little, Brown, 1979), 1346.
6. Nixon, *RN,* 700–701.
7. Kissinger, *The White House Years,* 1372.
8. Nixon, *RN,* 705.
9. Ibid., 766.
10. Kissinger, *The White House Years,* 1404.
11. Nixon, *RN,* 713.
12. Ibid., 717.
13. Kissinger, *The White House Years,* 1406.
14. Ibid.
15. Nixon, *RN,* 769.
16. Kissinger, *The White House Years,* 1408.

Chapter Seventeen

1. Stanley Karnow, *Vietnam: A History* (New York: Penguin Books, 1984, reprint of 1983 Viking Press edition), 654.
2. H. R. Haldeman with Joseph DiMona, *The Ends of Power* (New York: Times Books, 1978), 222.
3. Richard M. Nixon, *RN: The Memoirs of Richard Nixon* (New York: Grosset & Dunlap, 1978), 779.
4. Ibid., 799.

NOTES

181

5. *The Presidential Transcripts* (New York: Dell, 1974), 108.
6. Ibid., 99.
7. Ibid., 110.
8. Ibid., 140.
9. Nixon, *RN,* 801.
10. *The Presidential Transcripts,* 176.
11. Nixon, *RN,* 817.
12. Ibid., 827.
13. Ibid., 832.
14. Ibid., 847.
15. Ibid.
16. Ibid., 851.
17. Ibid., 893.

Chapter Eighteen

1. Richard M. Nixon, *RN: The Memoirs of Richard Nixon* (New York: Grosset & Dunlap, 1978), 903.
2. Ibid., 928.
3. Ibid., 935.
4. Theodore H. White, *Breach of Faith* (New York: Atheneum, 1975), 268.
5. Nixon, *RN,* 935.
6. Ibid., 971.

Chapter Nineteen

1. Richard M. Nixon, *RN: The Memoirs of Richard Nixon* (New York: Grosset & Dunlap, 1978), 989.
2. Theodore H. White, *Breach of Faith* (New York: Atheneum, 1975), 296.
3. Ibid., 297.
4. Ibid.
5. Nixon, *RN,* 996.
6. White, *Breach of Faith,* 4.
7. Nixon, *RN,* 1053.
8. Ibid., 1056.
9. Ibid., 1061.
10. Ibid., 1067–68.
11. Ibid., 1083.
12. Ibid., 1087.
13. Ibid., 1089.
14. Ibid., 1090.

Chapter Twenty

1. Julie Nixon Eisenhower, *Pat Nixon, the Untold Story* (New York: Simon and Schuster, 1986), 439.
2. Robert Sam Anson, *Exile: The Unquiet Oblivion of Richard M. Nixon* (New York: Simon and Schuster, 1984), 167.

NOTES

SOURCES

Ambrose, Stephen E. *Nixon: The Education of a Politician, 1913–1962.* New York: Simon and Schuster, 1987.

Anson, Robert Sam. *Exile: The Unquiet Oblivion of Richard M. Nixon.* New York: Simon and Schuster, 1984.

Bernstein, Carl, and Bob Woodward. *All the President's Men.* New York: Warner, 1975, reprint of 1974 Simon and Schuster edition.

Brodie, Fawn M. *Richard Nixon: The Shaping of His Character.* New York: Norton, 1981.

Dean, John W., III. *Blind Ambition: The White House Years.* New York: Simon and Schuster, 1976.

Ehrlichman, John. *Witness to Power.* New York: Simon and Schuster, 1982.

Eisenhower, Julie Nixon. *Pat Nixon, the Untold Story.* New York: Simon and Schuster, 1986.

From the President: Richard Nixon's Secret Files. Ed. Bruce Oudes. New York: Harper & Row, 1989.

Haldeman, H. R., with Joseph DiMona. *The Ends of Power.* New York: Times Books, 1978.

Karnow, Stanley. *Vietnam: A History.* New York: Penguin Books, 1984, reprint of 1983 Viking Press edition.

Kissinger, Henry. *The White House Years.* Boston: Little, Brown, 1979.

———*Years of Upheaval.* Boston: Little, Brown, 1982.

McGinnis, Joe. *The Selling of the President 1968.* New York: Pocket Books, 1970, reprint of 1969 Trident edition.

Nixon, Richard M. *RN: The Memoirs of Richard Nixon.* New York: Grosset & Dunlap, 1978.

Nixon, Richard M. *Six Crises.* New York: Doubleday, 1962.

The Presidential Transcripts. With commentary by the staff of the *Washington Post.* New York: Dell, 1974.

West, Jessamyn. *Hide and Seek: A Continuing Journey.* New York: Harcourt Brace Jovanovich, 1973.

White, Theodore H. *Breach of Faith: The Fall of Richard Nixon.* New York: Atheneum and Reader's Digest Press: 1975.

———. *The Making of the President 1960.* New York: Pocket Books, 1965, reprint of 1961 Atheneum edition.

———.*The Making of the President 1968.* New York: Atheneum, 1969.

———.*The Making of the President 1972.* New York: Bantam, 1973, reprint of 1973 Atheneum edition.

Woodward, Bob, and Carl Bernstein. *The Final Days.* New York: Simon and Schuster, 1976.

Wills, Garry. *Nixon Agonistes: The Crisis of a Self-Made Man.* Boston: Houghton Mifflin: 1970.

The Young Nixon: An Oral Inquiry. Ed. Renee K. Schulte. Fullerton: California State University, Oral History Program, 1978.

INTERVIEW BY AUTHOR

William Bagley, former campaign aide to Richard Nixon.

VIDEOTAPE

Tape of Richard Nixon's Checkers speech, on file at Indian Valley College, Novato, California.

SOURCES

INDEX

185

ABOUT THE AUTHOR

REBECCA LARSEN is a career newspaper journalist who currently works as an editor of the *Marin Independent Journal* in Marin County, California. She lives in Novato, California, with her husband, Alan, an accountant, and their three children. Rebecca Larsen's last two books for Franklin Watts were *Oppenheimer and the Atomic Bomb* and *Paul Robeson: Hero before His Time.*